THE Art OF CORPORATE SUCCESS

OTHER BOOKS BY KEN AULETTA

The Underclass
Hard Feelings
The Streets Were Paved with Gold

THE Art OF CORPORATE SUCCESS

The Story of Schlumberger

KEN AULETTA

G. P. Putnam's Sons / New York

Library of Congress Cataloging in Publication Data

Auletta, Ken.
The art of corporate success.

1. Schlumberger Limited—History. 2. Riboud, Jean,
1919–   .   I. Title.
HD9572.9.S34A94 1984   338.8'87   83-17749
ISBN 0-399-12930-8

Portions of this book originally appeared in *The New Yorker*.

PRINTED IN THE UNITED STATES OF AMERICA

FOR KATE

CONTENTS

The breath had been so pumped from my lungs as I went up that at the top I could go no farther, and sat down at once.

"Now you must free yourself from sloth," my mother said, "for, sitting on down or lying under covers, no one comes to fame . . . Therefore get up, overcome your panting with the spirit which wins every battle if it does not sink with its heavy body.

"A longer stairs must be climbed; it is not enough to have left this one."

Dante, The Divine Comedy

THE Art OF CORPORATE SUCCESS

INTRODUCTION

The first time I encountered the name Schlumberger or Jean Riboud was in the summer of 1981, which suggests either my ignorance or Schlumberger's low profile—or both. I stumbled across this quiet giant while hunting a company to profile for *The New Yorker* magazine. Back then, the travails of the American auto, steel, and smokestack industries crowded the news, and the frequently asked question was: Why is American industry failing? I set out to explore the flip side of that question: Why do companies succeed?

The first few months were spent asking people on Wall Street and elsewhere two simple questions: What's the best company in the world? And, what's the best company with an extraordinary chief executive?

I collected scores of candidates: established giants and brash newcomers; service, high-tech, and industrial companies; mammoth conglomerates with tentacles reaching into varied industries; and small, single-product firms. I eliminated well-known Goliaths that had already been profiled; corporate infants were removed because they had not yet proven their mettle; some corporations were lucky to be in the right business at the right time, and demonstrated no unusual qualities of leadership; others exhibited pluck but brought nothing innovative to the art of corporate success; a few interesting companies were led by uninteresting chief executives.

The process of elimination led me to Schlumberger and its chief executive, Jean Riboud. Schlumberger's performance had been spectacular over a period of many years, with the highest profit margin in 1981 of any of the world's 1000 leading industrial companies. It was in the high-tech information business, the leading growth industry of the late 20th century. It was multinational, reaching into ninety-two countries. It was founded by an unusual family, one that was concerned with advancing science as well as profits, one that worshiped the company as a religion and yet retained other passions, including art, politics, and civil rights. Finally, this was a company that for nineteen years had been steered by one man, Jean Riboud, a fiercely competitive capitalist who nevertheless calls himself a Socialist.

My editor at *The New Yorker*, William Shawn, approved the choice. In fact, Shawn was one of the few people I encountered outside the business community who knew of both Schlumberger and Riboud; most thought that Schlumberger was a jewelry concern. Shawn mentioned that years before, he had assigned a profile of Schlumberger to a writer, but the project had been dropped. I was eager to begin.

First, however, there were practical obstacles to overcome. Visits to the library revealed little about Schlumberger. A few stray pieces surfaced in business publications about the company's economic performance, but that was all. Schlumberger had a tradition of keeping journalists at a distance. Unlike Procter & Gamble, which spends more than $500 million annually on marketing—a sum that exceeds the profits of its nearest competitor, Colgate-Palmolive—Schlumberger is an intensely private company. It advertises, but only in the specialty press to show customers a new oil-well logging technique or to recruit engineers. There was no way to launch this assignment without their cooperation. And, initially, that cooperation was denied. I arranged to meet Riboud in New York, and told him simply that I would like to profile Schlumberger, not that I wished to profile one of the world's best companies. He said he would think on it. The next month I flew to Paris, spent several days with Riboud and his executives, and then, when I thought I had succeeded, Riboud said no. Schlumberger was doing fine without publicity, thank you.

I was in so deep that I persisted, and after a few more rejections Riboud relented. Why?

My guess is that several factors conspired, the most important being my association with *The New Yorker*. Over the years Riboud had been an intimate of many *New Yorker* contributors—A. J. Liebling, Joseph Mitchell, Saul Steinberg, Peter Taylor, among others—and read the magazine regularly. He equated *The New Yorker* with Schlumberger—each was the best at what it did. One of my problems was that I was not Joe Liebling. Over lunch in the small dining room adjoining his office, as we emptied a bottle of Lynch Bages and sampled an assortment of French cheeses, Riboud observed matter-of-factly that I did not write as well as Liebling, did not have his eye. *What a wonderful profile Liebling could have written*, Riboud said, wistfully. *Joe could have captured the nuance of Schlumberger, its special spirit.*

I let it pass, pretending that Riboud was paying tribute to Liebling, rather than trying to send me a message. Because Riboud was comfortable with *The New Yorker*, knew it did not lust for headlines or gossip, finally he relented. He was probably swayed by other factors as well. After years of anonymity, he may have wanted an audience to appreciate Schlumberger, which Riboud calls "the best company in the world." He could not imagine that a visitor would fail to be impressed by his beloved company. And as he neared the mandatory retirement age of sixty-five and rumors mounted that he would join the government of his friend President François Mitterrand, Riboud was becoming a bit less press shy; perhaps he would even benefit from public exposure. One does not rise to the peak of any profession uncursed by vanity. Finally, Riboud and I developed a relaxed relationship; if you're going to risk making a fool of yourself, why not enjoy it.

Once he agreed, Riboud sent a memorandum notifying Schlumberger executives that he was cooperating with a *New Yorker* writer and urging them to speak with me. Over the course of the next year, I interviewed many of these executives, attended meetings, read internal memorandums, made field visits with Riboud, sat quietly like a fly on the wall of his office, stayed in a Schlumberger camp in the Egyptian desert, and engaged Riboud in perhaps one hundred hours of conversation. Although Riboud erected an impenetrable wall when he wished to keep me from a meeting or from inspecting a document, he and his associates were uncommonly generous. When I had difficulty reaching several of his critics in France, Riboud helped arrange interviews. Twice over the course of a long weekend at La Carelle, he drove me to the home of his sister Françoise—with whom he hardly speaks—leaving me twice to ring a front doorbell that went unanswered.

The two-part profile of Riboud and Schlumberger appeared in June of 1983. In preparing these articles for book publication, I have used June 1983 as my cutoff date, collecting no new factual material after that date. I have also expanded the profile, adding 15 to 20 percent more material.

In the end I came to believe that Riboud is an unusual executive not just because he rules his company with perhaps as free a hand as any chief executive of a public company, but because many of the people in his employ feel free to express independent opinions. Riboud, as was said of Samuel Johnson, is a man who "temperamentally" is "always in revolt," and that temperament—one that was also possessed by Marcel Schlumberger, who recruited Riboud—is part of the Schlumberger culture. Schlumberger is a company that combines a tradition of pride for past achievements with the humility that comes from a recognition that there are more stairs to climb; a company that is self-confident without being smug. Competition and being kept on one's toes is the norm. Because Schlumberger dominates the oilfield-service industry, it is difficult for employees to feel the hot breath of competition. To compensate, Schlumberger constantly emphasizes that they are in a service business, reminding employees that they must serve others. To combat arrogance, Riboud regularly "shakes the tree," transferring or terminating executives, instilling a perpetual sense of competition and insecurity. Further, he sets a standard that is impossible to meet. It is not enough to be the best, to be number one, Riboud says often. A great company must strive for perfection.

This philosophy has helped keep Schlumberger from becoming inbred, self-satisfied, as it is said the Polaroid Corporation became; it has prevented Schlumberger employees from becoming too secure, like legions of civil servants. Schlumberger is no Bendix, its executives preoccupied with devising "golden parachutes" to protect themselves from corporate takeovers; nor is Schlumberger overrun with lawyers, the latest management methodologies from the Harvard Business School, or endless paper flow. It is not fixated, as too many American corporations are, by quarterly profit statements and short-term paper results, a fixation that envelops companies in unproductive debt and saps entrepreneurial spirit. The idea of merit pay and rewards for performance is critical to the workings of a company like Schlumberger, as it should be to the American teaching profession. Decentralized management is a way of life at Schlumberger, one that is as alien to many large corporations as it is to governments. And Schlumberger's products "sell" because they are of quality, not because they are packaged cleverly by Madison Avenue. In short, there is much that students of business, not to mention government managers, can learn from the art of corporate success at Schlumberger.

There is a literature of romance about corporations. As seasons change, so do theories about what determines success. We embrace and fall in love with business techniques, creating fads. The secret to corporate success was once thought to be found in William H. Whyte's "organization man" or David Riesman's "other directed" man, corporate types who rose because they were cautious bureaucrats. A few years ago Michael Maccoby's "gamesman," a more daring risk-taker, was boiler-plated as the model for success. From Japan we have fallen in love with "Theory Z," with the cooperative spirit between management and labor there. The latest rage—spurred by a recent bestseller, *In Search of Excellence*, by Thomas J. Peters and Robert H. Waterman, Jr.—is that the secret ingredient for success is a distinctive "corporate culture."

In truth, a company like Schlumberger contains a variety of individuals; a kaleidoscope of factors converge to shape its success. Schlumberger has its share of Babbitts and "gamesmen." In fact, sometimes the two opposite qualities reside within the same individual. No single management theory explains its success.

A company like Schlumberger succeeds both because it understands the art of corporate success, has fashioned its own distinct culture, and because it practices the science of management, including the willingness to pour its treasure into technological research.

Alone, a strong corporate culture may not be enough to fortify a company against cheaper competition from abroad. The Arab oil embargo and the resulting rise in gasoline prices devastated the American auto industry perhaps as much as Detroit's shortsighted executives. The cooperative spirit permeating Japanese industry is more difficult to replicate in an ethnically and racially diverse America, a nation less worshipful of authority, more attuned to checks and balances, including the now traditional check of a strong union. Nor is the latest totem—that American companies have been eclipsed by the Japanese—a full portrait of corporate reality. The American corporate success story, as Peters and Waterman remind readers, is no dinosaur. IBM, Hewlett-Packard, Coca-Cola, and Procter & Gamble, among others, do not walk in the shadow of Sony or Hitachi.

A few years ago I spent time exploring America's underclass, a group of Americans fearful of, or hostile to, organized society. I came away from my encounter with street criminals, hustlers, the hard-core unemployed, long-term welfare recipients and their teenage daughters and fatherless sons, with a conviction that the "science" of government—passing laws, devising programs, spending money—alone will not defuse this domestic atom bomb. In trying to understand why some people succeed and others fail, I came away convinced that while government has a crucial role, we too often neglect the role played by values—by those unmeasurable, unquantifiable qualities of character, ambition, faith, self-confidence. By what might be called the art of self-improvement. I came away from my study of Schlumberger convinced that intangible qualities also play a crucial role in determining which companies succeed.

I am not a long-term student of business, but my encounter with Schlumberger suggests that the world's great companies may share at least some common qualities, beyond a quality product. They tend to be entrepreneurial rather than managerial; they have faith in a future vision, and stick to it; they resolve the tension between authority and participation in such a way that employees feel as if it is their company, and yet feel a part of something larger than themselves; they feel secure that they are the best, yet insecure because they are not perfect.

Perhaps this tradition of striving for perfection is what most separates the great from the merely good companies, just as it distinguishes the great baseball teams, a great symphony orchestra, university, or nation. Talent alone does not define greatness. A less tangible spirit is at work, driving a company like Schlumberger up the "longer stairs that must be climbed . . ."

1

THE QUIET GIANT

From the windows of Jean Riboud's New York office, on the forty-fourth floor at 277 Park Avenue, one can see the buildings that house the headquarters of such corporate giants as Warner Communications, Gulf + Western, Citicorp, International Telephone and Telegraph, Colgate-Palmolive, United Brands, Bankers Trust, CBS, RCA, and International Paper. All of them are better known than Schlumberger Limited, the company that Riboud is chairman and chief executive officer of, but none of them can match Schlumberger's profits. In stock-market value—the number of outstanding shares multiplied by the price per share—only three companies were worth more than Schlumberger at the end of 1981. They were AT & T ($48 billion), IBM ($34 billion), and Exxon ($27 billion). Schlumberger was then worth $16 billion. In 1982 it was worth about $17 billion.

Riboud has offices in New York and Paris, and both are rather ordinary except for the art on the walls— works by Picasso, Klee, Max Ernst, Magritte, Jasper Johns, Victor Brauner, Janez Bernik. His New York office is a snug corner—sixteen feet by twenty—with beige walls. An adjoining conference room, seventeen feet by eighteen, has one couch and a round wooden table with six chairs. Riboud's office has a single telephone with just two lines, and no private bathroom; there are white blinds on the windows, and a simple beige sisal carpet on the floor. His desk is a long, rectangular teak table with chrome legs; on it are a few memorandums but no "in" or "out" box and no books. His personal New York staff consists of one secretary, Lucille Northrup, to whom he rarely dictates; memorandums and paperwork are frowned upon at Schlumberger, and when Riboud wants to send out a memorandum he first writes it in longhand. His Paris office is equally uncluttered.

Riboud is sixty-three years old. He is five feet ten inches tall and slight of build, with wavy gray hair combed straight back. His nose is long and thin, his lips are narrow. His suits come in conservative shades, and his shirts are usually quiet solid colors. He speaks softly, sometimes almost inaudibly, in accented English, rarely gesticulates, and is an intense listener, usually inspecting his long fingers while others speak. Everything about Riboud conveys an impression of delicacy except his eyes, which are deep brown and cryptic. He arrives at work around 10 A.M., and he takes at least six weeks' vacation annually. Yet he is no figurehead; rather, he believes in delegating authority—a principle that no doubt accounts for the calm of Schlumberger's offices in New York and Paris. Schlumberger employs 75,000 people, and of that number only 197 work at the two headquarters.

In many respects—some obvious and some not so obvious—Riboud is not a typical business executive. As a young man in Lyons, he flirted with Communism and railed against Franco, Fascism, and the French establishment, including the Roman Catholic Church. During the Second World War, he joined the Resistance; he was captured in 1943 and sent to Buchenwald. Almost two years later, when he emerged, he had tuberculosis and weighed ninety-six pounds. Riboud will talk about his wartime ordeal only with great reluctance. He has never discussed it with his wife, Krishna, who was born in India, or with his closest friends, who, over the years, have included the writers Lillian Hellman, A. J. Liebling, Jean Stafford, and Langston Hughes; the artists Max Ernst (Riboud is the executor of Ernst's estate), Victor Brauner, Saul Steinberg, and Roberto Matta; the photographers Henri Cartier-Bresson, Robert Capa, and David (Chim) Seymour; the composer John Cage; the filmmaker Roberto Rossellini and the film historian Henri Langlois, who founded the Cinémathèque Française, the world's first film museum; and a procession of important political figures on the French left, including former Prime Minister Pierre Mendès-France, the writer and editor Jean-Jacques Servan-Schreiber, and President François Mitterrand. The one friend he has discussed his wartime experiences with is the American poet and critic Charles Olson, who dedicated his 1950 prose poem "The Resistance" to Riboud, and who also served as best man at Krishna and Jean Riboud's wedding.

As the chief executive of a multinational corporation—Schlumberger does business in ninety-two countries—Riboud (pronounced "Ree-boo") has a somewhat surprising talent for avoiding publicity. He is a stranger to most other corporate executives, deliberately keeping his distance from them. He sits on no other company's board of directors. He seldom ventures from his office for lunch or from his home for dinner. If he does accept a dinner invitation, his host may find him sincere, solicitous, charming—and realize later that he has volunteered virtually nothing about himself. When he goes on business trips, he prefers to stay with friends rather than at hotels. Riboud sometimes vacations at a house he owns in the Arizona desert and, more frequently, at his family's estate—a château near the village of Ouroux, in the Beaujolais region.

Riboud, who says that he remains loyal to the Socialism of his youth, has been the chief executive of Schlumberger for almost nineteen years. Because the corporation does no mass advertising, of either the consumer or the institutional sort, because it retains no lobbyist in Washington and no public-relations agency in New York or Paris, and because it has never been involved in a public controversy, Schlumberger (pronounced "shlum-bare-zhay") remains one of the world's quiet giants. It is a high-technology company that generates the bulk of its income from the oilfield-service business—making tools that enable oil companies to find and drill for oil with great precision. The information gained and the techniques learned in oilfield services have helped the company to expand into such fields as electric, gas, and water meters; flight-test systems; transformers and semiconductors; automatic test equipment for integrated-circuit chips; electronic telephone circuits; computer-aided design and manufacturing processes; and robotics. On Main Street, those who've heard of Schlumberger sometimes think of the jewelry firm of the same name (no relation). But Schlumberger is recognized on Wall Street as one of the world's best-managed multinational companies, and financial analysts can point to a number of facts to document its success. Its net income has grown by about 30 percent in each of the past ten years up to 1981. Its earnings per share rose by more than 30 percent annually between 1971 and 1981, even though the price of oil remained stable or declined in several of those years. Its net profits in 1982 totaled $1.35 billion on revenues of $6.284 billion, for a profit as a percentage of revenue of 21 percent—higher than that of any of the thousand other leading industrial companies in the world. Its return on equity in 1981 was 34 percent, while the median for the Fortune 500 companies was 13.8 percent. Schlumberger has relatively little long-term debt: it amounted to just $462 million at the end of 1982, or 8 percent of the company's total capitalization. And while the profits of most oil and oilfield-service companies fell sharply in 1982, Schlumberger's net income rose by more than 6 percent.

Science is the foundation of Schlumberger. Science is the link between the various corporate subsidiaries, for the task of most of them is collecting, measuring, and transmitting data. Science, and particularly geophysics, was at the core of the careers of Conrad and Marcel Schlumberger, the company's founders. Both were born in the town of Guebwiller, in Alsace—Conrad in 1878 and Marcel six years later. They were two of six children of a Protestant family that owned a prosperous textile machine business. Their mother, Marguerite de Witt, was a feminist who was head of the International Woman Suffrage Alliance after the First World War. Their father, Paul, was a visionary with a rocklike faith in science and in projects like the Suez Canal, in which he was an early investor. A great-grandfather, François Guizot, was prime minister of France from 1840 to 1848, during the reign of Louis Philippe.

Conrad Schlumberger, who fought in the First World War, read the letters of dead German soldiers and was so moved that he became a lifelong pacifist; he identified with Socialists, and was a financial backer of the French Socialist—now Communist—newspaper *L'Humanité*. His great passion, however, was science, and in 1893 he left home to study physics at the École Polytechnique, in Paris. After graduation, he taught physics at the École des Mines, in Paris, while trying to figure out how to use electricity to make measurements of the earth's subsurface—something that had never been done. His brother Marcel was more an "adapter" than an inventor—a tough-minded, pragmatic man with absolutely no interest in politics, who went to Paris to study civil engineering at L'École Centrale des Arts et Manufactures. Conrad was outgoing and passionate, and a scientific genius. Marcel was shy and cautious, and a shrewd businessman. Still, the two brothers were very close.

Paul Schlumberger, seeing his sons' complementary talents, and frustrated because the textile machine factory had sidetracked his own scientific ambitions, abandoned the business to his brothers, packed up his family, and moved to Paris to be near Conrad and Marcel. He persuaded them to merge their talents and form a partnership with him, to pursue Conrad's theory about measuring the earth's subsurface. He would provide as much as half a million francs to support the undertaking. On November 12, 1919, the three men signed an agreement, written by Paul Schlumberger, that said:

> For their part my sons agree not to dilute their efforts by working in other areas . . . In this undertaking, the interests of scientific research take precedence over financial ones. I will be kept informed of, and may give my opinion on, important developments and the necessary expenses required. The money given by me is my contribution to a work primarily scientific and secondarily practical . . . Marcel will bring to Conrad his remarkable ability as an engineer and his common sense. Conrad, on the other hand, will be the man of science. I will support them.

Over the next several years, relying on Conrad's scientific creativity and Marcel's practical engineering skills, the Schlumberger brothers pursued Conrad's theory that by charting the electrical resistivity of various rock formations and then comparing the patterns, they would in effect be able to draw a picture of what lay beneath the earth's surface. The theory proved correct, and the brothers made the first discoveries by surface electrical measurement of iron ore, copper, and an oil-producing salt dome. In the mid-twenties, however, there was no demand for their services, so the partners took no sal-

ary, lived modestly, and counseled their employees—
they had five when they started—to be patient.

Their breakthrough came in 1927, when a director
of the Péchelbronn Oil Company, in Alsace, asked
whether their technique could be used in searching for
oil, which usually migrates through such porous rocks
as limestone and sandstone until it is trapped by im-
permeable rock. Ever since the first oil well was drilled,
in 1859, oil companies had longed for a technology that
would help them find oil. Initially, prospectors had to
painstakingly extract core samples and drill cuttings
from rock formations, haul them slowly to the surface,
ship them to a laboratory, and await a chemical analysis. This tedious, expensive process enabled the oil
companies to determine whether there was oil in a given
area, and even to determine its quality; but not its precise quantity, or the exact shape of the well, and it did
not enable them to pinpoint where to drill. Conrad,
having discovered a new geophysical principle, assigned the job of fashioning a tool and testing it to Henri
Doll, who was a brilliant young engineer and also the
husband of Conrad's daughter Anne. Doll's task was to
chart the electric current as it encountered various kinds
of rock, water, and oil. By comparing the actual current
coursing through the earth with records showing the
electrical resistivity of each substance, the brothers and
Doll hoped to produce what amounted to the world's
first X ray of an oil well. Their site was selected—a
small oilfield at Péchelbronn, not far from where the
Schlumbergers had grown up. The crucial test took place
on a clear day in late summer. In a battered station
wagon, Conrad Schlumberger, along with Doll and two
other engineers, went to the site. They attached a measuring device called a sonde to a cable and snaked it
down into a fifteen-hundred-foot hole. In an oral history
of Schlumberger prepared by the company in 1977, Doll
described the device that was to transform the oil business:

We made a sonde by connecting four meter-long sections of Bakelite tubing together by means of short lengths of brass tubing, fastening them to each other with brass screws. The electrodes were wired to the Bakelite tubes. We contrived a weight, or plummet, for the bottom of the sonde, making it of one meter of brass tubing, four centimeters in diameter, and filling it with lead pellets like those used in duck shooting. It was plugged at both ends and weighed about twenty-five pounds. The whole assembly looked like a long black snake with five joints.

The cable, if you could call it that, was three lengths of rubber-insulated copper wire, like the kind used on spark plugs in cars. It had a tensile strength of about eight pounds per wire. The wires weren't spliced together, as was done in later surveys, but were allowed to wind onto the winch drum loose from each other.

The winch had an X-shaped wooden frame; the drum was made with wooden flanges and the core of a large Bakelite tube. It was assembled by long brass bars and nuts. To turn the drum, we had a big pinion connected to a smaller pinion by a motorcycle chain. The moving axle was steel, with a bicycle pedal mounted at either end. One of us would get on one side and one on the other, and turn the pedals. There was a ratchet to keep the drum from unwinding.

We had no collector. Instead, we had a plug, much like a common wall plug, at the side of the winch flange. When the winch had to be turned, the cable connection to the potentiometer was unplugged so the turn could be made. Then the cable was plugged back in so that we could make the readings.

The sheave was made of wood with an eccentric axle. It had a long tail as a counterbalance. This

served as our strain gauge. We were very worried
about the wires breaking, and by watching the
rise and fall of the tail, you could tell what kind
of pull was being exerted on the wires. For depth
measurement, we had a counter on the sheave
wheel like the mileage indicator on a car. We
planned to take readings at intervals of one meter.

We made our measurements with a standard
potentiometer mounted on a tripod like those we
used in our surface exploration work.

To take the measurements, one of the men unplugged
the connector, one turned the winch, one ran up on the
rig floor to inspect the counter on the sheave. Doll wrote
down the measurements and depth readings on a pad.
They hurried to unplug, roll up the cable, and rush to
the next point, where the process was repeated—one
meter at a time. At the end of the day, exhausted and
caked with mud, they went to a nearby village to bathe
and celebrate. Doll returned to Paris, where he plotted
the various readings on graph paper. On September 5,
1927, Doll produced the first electrical-resistance log.

Doll and the Schlumberger brothers were ecstatic,
expecting oil companies to line up for the services of
their company—the Société de Prospection Électrique,
know as Pros. That did not happen. French oil companies were wary of turning over their secrets to an
outside service company, and non-French companies
suspected that these three unknown Frenchmen were
quacks. Two fallow years passed before the Schlumberger brothers captured their first major client—the
Soviet Union. For Conrad, it was like a dream come
true. He had believed in the Socialist Revolution, and
now he felt vindicated. A Communist government—
the only one in existence—was looking ahead, unsus-
picious, unparochial. Several years later, American oil
companies began to follow suit.

Today, the tools are more refined, but the basic process—wireline logging, as it came to be known—is a measurement taken on just about every oil or gas well drilled in the world. And today, without benefit of a patent on its basic logging process, Schlumberger—as the original partnership was renamed in 1934—has a near-monopoly on this business, logging some 70 percent of the world's wells. In the United States alone, in 1981 the company hired 1 percent of all the engineers graduating from American colleges.

Over the years, Schlumberger's oilfield business has expanded beyond logging measurements to include a broad range of other services: drilling, testing, and completing wells; pumping; cementing. The company's Forex Neptune subsidiary, formed in the 1960s, is now the world's largest oil-drilling company. The Johnston-Macco and Flopetrol subsidiaries provide an assortment of testing and completion services after drilling has started. A subsidiary called The Analysts provides continuous detailed logs of oil wells from the moment drilling begins, in contrast to wireline logs, which are prepared only before drilling begins or after it ceases. The Dowell Schlumberger company, which is jointly owned by Schlumberger and Dow Chemical, offers pumping and cementing services. Together with the Wireline division, these companies make up the Oilfield Services—one of two major parts of the Schlumberger empire. The other major part is known as Measurement, Control & Components. Its subsidiaries include the world's largest manufacturer of electric, gas, and water meters; a leading manufacturer of transformers; a producer of valves and safety controls for nuclear power systems; and a manufacturer of flight-control and signal-processing systems for aerospace and military use. The Fairchild Camera & Instrument Corporation, a California-based semiconductor company that Schlumberger acquired in 1979, manufactures, among other products, integrated circuits such as microprocessors and memories; advanced bipolar microprocessors for the F-16 fighter plane; and electronic telephone circuits. Applicon, another subsidiary, is among the pioneers in computer-aided design and other efforts to automate factories.

Schlumberger has a total of forty-three major subsidiaries, most of which rely on science and technology. The jewel in Schlumberger's crown is the Wireline, which in 1982 generated 45 percent of the company's $6.284 billion in revenues and about 70 percent of its $1.35 billion in net profits. Many of Schlumberger's subsidiaries rank at or near the top of their various industries. The investment banker Felix Rohatyn, who serves on the boards of eight major corporations, including Schlumberger, and is a close friend of Riboud's, says, "By the standard of profit margins, return on investment, compound growth rate, of remaining ahead of the state of the art technically and having an efficient management structure, over the last twenty years—until the recent drastic change in the energy environment— Schlumberger might well have been the single best business in the world." Rohatyn's enthusiasm is shared by independent analysts at the major Wall Street brokerage firms, and their judgment has been reflected in research reports issued by, among others, Morgan Stanley, Merrill Lynch, Paine Webber, Wertheim, and L. F. Rothschild Unterberg Towbin. An analysis issued by Barton M. Biggs, managing director of Morgan Stanley in January of 1982 reads, "Here is this immense, superbly—almost artistically—managed company booming along with a 35 percent compound annual growth rate in earnings and 37 percent in dividends between 1975 and 1980 . . . Our analysis of earnings variability from growth trend shows Schlumberger as having the most consistent, high-growth track of any company in the 1400-stock universe of our dividend discount model."

2

JEAN RIBOUD: THE EARLY YEARS

Even though Schlumberger is a competitive company devoted to ever-higher profits, over the years its executives have shown a predilection for the politics of the left. Paul Schlumberger urged his sons to share the profits of their company with employees. He financed his sons only on the condition that "the interests of scientific research take precedence over financial ones." Conrad was a pacifist and a romantic socialist until Stalin's Russia disillusioned him. René Seydoux, the husband of Marcel's daughter Geneviève, who ran Schlumberger's European wireline operations, and to whom Riboud reported after Marcel's death, in 1953, was an ardent and active supporter of the French Socialist Party. Jean de Ménil, who supervised all South American operations in the period after the Second World War, supported various liberal causes in the United States. His wife, Dominique, a daughter of Conrad Schlumberger, became an important financial contributor first to the American civil-rights movement and later to black and Hispanic candidates for office. And in 1981 Jean Riboud, as an intimate of President Mitterrand, supported the Socialist government's proposed nationalization of forty-six enterprises.

Riboud is a man of contrasts. He is a hugely successful capitalist, with an annual salary of $700,000
and Schlumberger stock worth about $35 million, yet
he calls himself a Socialist. He loves business, yet most
of his friends are from the worlds of art and politics.
He was born into a French banking family in Lyons,
one of the historical birthplaces of the French ruling
class, yet he says a principal goal in his life is to battle
this class. He has deep roots in France, yet he considers
himself an unofficial citizen of India and of the United
States. He places a premium on loyalty and sentiment,
yet he is a tough businessman who has unhesitatingly
fired loyal executives and has had a hand in easing out
four members of the Schlumberger family. He is charming yet distant. He is a strong and independent man,
yet he has a history of "more or less falling in love"—
in the words of his friend the writer Françoise Giroud—
with leading French politicians of the left.

Even to many of his friends, Riboud is an enigma.
They do not understand his success as a capitalist—in
part because he does not speak of Schlumberger to them.
"Jean Riboud impersonates a businessman who is trying
to hide a certain poetry," Saul Steinberg says. "He is
in some sort of Sydney Greenstreet business, as far as
we see it—oil, Arabia. I say, 'What's this pussycat doing
as director of this company? I can see the pussycat. But
where is the crocodile?' Now, no pussycat becomes
officer in charge of such a company, and I tell myself
that in order to be good on the highest level of anything
you need mysterious sources."

Few cities dominate nations the way Lyons once
dominated France. A city of over half a million people
in the center of France, Lyons was synonymous with
the French business establishment. The Ribouds were
Roman Catholic—the right religion—and comfortable.
The family lived in an apartment in Lyons until 1929,

when they moved to a spacious house in the suburb of Écully. Summers were spent fifty-five miles north of Lyons, at La Carelle, an estate of 1300 acres of farmland and wooded hills, which has been in the family since 1850. Like many members of the French establishment, Camille Riboud, Jean's father, attended the École des Sciences Politiques, in Paris, where his circle of friends included Georges Boris, who became a close associate of Pierre Mendès-France; André Istel, a future banker; Maurice Schlumberger, who became a banking partner of Istel's; and Jean Schlumberger, who became a writer of some distinction. Maurice and Jean Schlumberger were brothers of Conrad and Marcel. After Camille Riboud and Maurice Schlumberger graduated from the École des Sciences Politiques, their parents gave them an eighteen-month trip around the world, which they embarked on in 1910. The bond between Camille and Maurice deepened, and years later they would often take their children on trips together—hiking in Corsica, skiing in the French Alps.

Camille returned to Lyons in 1912, with dreams of becoming a professor of literature, but his father, who was a banker with the Société Lyonnaise de Dépôts, wanted his son to be a banker, too, and Camille obeyed. Secretly, he disdained many of his banking associates— especially those who were "the son of," Antoine Riboud, Camille's eldest son, recalls. Many of his close friends were professors from Lyons universities. Unlike most of his banking colleagues, Camille was not "of the right." Nor was he "of the left." Jean Riboud says, "My father was an enlightened conservative. He was really part of the establishment and wanted to be part of the establishment, and yet he wanted to be entirely independent-minded—independent of the establishment." His days were devoted to commerce. At night, he read to his children: Homer, Euripides, Baudelaire, Verlaine, Rimbaud. Camille Rimboud was a man of contrasts, of masks.

Camille's wife, Hélène, was a simpler person. She grew up in Lyons, and spent her summers in the nearby town of Givors, where her father's family owned a bottling factory. Hélène Riboud was taught to be a devout, unquestioning Catholic, to obey her husband, to control her emotions, and to organize a good home. She "was not a silly woman,"Antoine Riboud says, but she was "ordinary"—without "the sparkle of my father." Jean Riboud offers a different memory of Hélène. "She was a lively, attractive, gay woman, without the culture of my father," he says. "But she was not an ordinary person." The qualities that Jean remembers most vividly are "an extraordinary dignity and an extraordinary sense of duty." Krishna Riboud remembers her mother-in-law, who died in 1957, as a woman of "great determination and great character," but she also says that Jean has a romanticized view of his father. "He feels that all his cultural background comes from his father," she says. "All the authority he has comes from the mother. I see more of the mother in him than the father."

Hélène and Camille Riboud were married in 1915 and had seven children—four boys and three girls. The firstborn was a daughter, Michèle. Then came Antoine, a sickly child, who spent part of his youth in sanatoriums. The Ribouds had a second son eleven months later, on November 15, 1919, and named him Jean. Because they feared that Antoine would not survive, they treated Jean as the eldest child. He was the favored son, and his parents expected him to guide the older Michèle and Antoine as well as the younger children— Françoise, Sylvie, Marc, and Olivier. (Olivier died of scarlet fever at eleven.) While Antoine struggled in school, Jean was an outstanding student and also a good athlete. He was voted the "best liked" in high school and was made Boy Scout leader for the entire Lyons region. Of all the Riboud children, Jean and his sister Françoise, who were close, especially enjoyed listening to their father read aloud at night; they liked meeting his friends and discussing art, literature, and politics. Influenced by the books they read, by the ideas discussed by the university men, and perhaps by their father's own opinions, Jean and Françoise became the most political of the children, and by the time they reached their teens they were denouncing the people who ruled their church and their city as "the little Fascist bourgeoisie." In 1936, they ardently embraced Léon Blum's Popular Front government and its thirteen-month effort to bring about social change in France. They vehemently opposed Hitler, Franco, and the Munich pact.

In 1939, at the age of fifty-three, Camille Riboud died of a heart attack, and Jean, who was then nineteen, became the de facto head of the family. "Jean is exactly the portrait, the figure of my father," Antoine Riboud says. "He has the same intellectual way of thinking as my father. To all the children, he was the second father. Sometimes too much, even with Françoise. Sometimes too much with Marc. The only one who had no interference in his life was Antoine. I never had problems with my brother." Perhaps because Jean was seen as assuming too much authority, perhaps because he can be cold, some lasting resentments were created. Marc Riboud, who is now a world-famous photographer, and Jean speak to each other only to be polite. Michèle, who is now a Paris housewife, until recently had little contact with her brother. Antoine and Jean consult on business matters, and like and respect each other, but are not close. Françoise, who today runs a school and home for handicapped children at La Carelle, has been distant from Jean since 1977, when she challenged his slate in a local election and won the seat on the village council which he had held since shortly after the war. Of all his sisters and brothers, the closest to Jean is Sylvie, who is a housewife in Aix-en-Provence.

With the approach of the Second World War, Antoine married and entered his maternal grandfather's bottling factory. There he spent the war years, eventually taking over. He had a flair for marketing and sales, and transformed the bottling company into BSN–Gervais Danone—a multinational rival of such corporations as Nestlé SA and General Foods. Its products include, in addition to bottles and glass, Dannon yogurt, Kronenbourg beer, Évian water, soft drinks, pasta, mustards, baby foods, and plastics.

Although both head multinational companies, the brothers are unalike. Physically, Antoine is the same height as Jean but heavier, with a bulky, flatter nose. He wears flashier suits, slaps people on the back, laughs heartily. The essential Antoine Riboud is contained in a story he tells of how American authorities would not permit him to export a Chardonnay wine—Cuvée des Copains Spécial—he grows on his farm near the Swiss border. Antoine's answer was that of a skilled marketing man: he outsmarted customs officials by pouring the same wine into a different bottle. He invented a new package. His brother Jean would probably have invented a new product.

Whereas Antoine was cheerfully nonpolitical, Jean felt that he could not escape choices. In 1939, after graduating from the École des Sciences Politiques, he volunteered for the Army but was rejected, because, at nineteen, he was too young. The next year, though, he joined the Army as a tank officer, and when Germany invaded France he was sent into battle in the Loire Valley. He was captured in June of 1940, but he escaped. In the spring of 1941, he went to the Sorbonne to study law and economics and prepare for the Civil Service. He studied and lived for two years in occupied Paris, and during this time he kept in touch with the budding Resistance movement in Lyons, attending organizational meetings and slipping back and forth between occupied France and Vichy France.

In the summer of 1943 he and a fellow student, Yves Le Portz, were urged by others in the Resistance to join the Free French Army in North Africa. To get there, they decided to take a route that had been used by, among others, Georges Schlumberger, a son of Maurice: to Perpignan, in the south, by bicycle, and from there the twenty-five miles or so to Spain by kayak. On a moonless August night, Riboud and Le Portz hid their bicycles at the top of a cliff, put their kayak into the water, and paddled furiously, hoping to parallel the coastline just out of sight. But a storm came up, sending water crashing into their tiny craft and shoving them out into rough seas. Frantically, they struggled back toward the shore, where the water was calmer, and then they made their way south, to a point where the Pyrenees plunged straight down into the Mediterranean. They spotted a cave and, leaving their kayak outside, crawled in to sleep. When they awoke, Riboud recalls, "two men were looking at us, and they were obviously totally baffled." The two men happened to be German naval officers. Riboud and Le Portz pretended to be students. The Germans stared at them and departed without saying a word. Riboud and Le Portz went back to sleep. They were awakened a short while later by officers from a German patrol boat, who, after one look at the detailed maps of the coast of Spain the two were carrying, arrested them. The Germans took them to be interrogated by a colonel, who first saluted their bravery and then turned them over to the Gestapo in Perpignan. After two weeks of questioning, they were taken to the city of Compiègne, north of Paris, and in September they were among 1200 prisoners shipped by train to Buchenwald.

When Riboud and Le Portz arrived at Buchenwald, experienced prisoners gave them some advice: The Gestapo will ask if you are able to do mechanical work. Say yes. "We had no idea of mechanics at all," recalls Le Portz, who is today chairman of the European Investment Bank. But they followed the advice, and were sent to an aircraft-construction plant near Buchenwald.

Prisoners who said they were ignorant of mechanics were sent on to Dora, an extermination camp. Buchenwald was brutal—particularly the long hours working outdoors in winter without a coat. In addition to the cold, the hard labor, and the Gestapo, prisoners of war had to contend with common criminals whom the Germans had rounded up and sent to the camps. "To divide us, they mixed ordinary criminals with members of the Resistance," Le Portz says. "There were as many conflicts among inmates as between inmates and guards. Unity among the prisoners was essential."

Riboud recalls that in many of the camps "some of the Christians and the Communists became forces of order." They helped their fellow prisoners not to lose faith, and to accept discipline and solidarity. Riboud himself soon emerged as a leader at Buchenwald. "We didn't speak German," Le Portz says. "Yet a few months after entering the camp Jean was the official German interpreter for the prisoners—and he'd read German newspapers to them. Moreover, he was a man of extraordinary courage and humor. He tried to make life as easy as possible for other prisoners. Jean managed to establish contact with the outside world and get information to the camp. He was not a passive man."

Riboud's brother Antoine and his friend Cartier-Bresson have said that Riboud emerged from the camp thinking of himself as a Communist, although not in the sense of being a Party member or a Stalinist. "I was never tempted at all to become a Party member," Riboud says. He does concede, however, that it took him "a long time to realize the force of destruction that was Stalin," explaining, "I couldn't believe that people I'd known in Buchenwald—who had convictions, and integrity—could have lent themselves to an evil like Stalinism." Of his years at Buchenwald, Riboud says, "I've seen the worst and the best of human beings, to an extent that I never thought could be as bad and as good, as ominous and as perfect." The experience contributed to a lifelong conviction that, in Riboud's words, "in the presence of death there are the ones who fight and the ones who give up, the ones who survive and the ones who do not." Antoine Riboud says that Buchenwald made his brother "more liberal" and also made him "very strong, very capable of resisting anything."

When Buchenwald was liberated, on April 11, 1945, only ninety-two of the 1200 prisoners who had been on the train from Compiègne were still alive. Two days later, some French nationals arrived to interview the prisoners, and were horrified by what they learned. They chose a delegation of five prisoners, including Riboud, and rushed them to Paris by plane to give officials an account of their ordeal. They received a hero's welcome, after which Riboud took a train from Paris to Lyons, and from there traveled on to La Carelle. All 400 residents of the village of Ouroux turned out to greet him, and he stayed up through the night drinking wine with them at the village café, and singing. Riboud never forgot the bond he felt with the people of Ouroux. Some time later, he was elected a member of the village council, and he attended two or three meetings a year until his defeat in 1977.

A career in banking had been Camille Riboud's wish for Jean, and though Jean had no ambitions along those lines he decided to fall in with his father's plan. With the war behind him, Jean assumed that a job in his father's bank awaited him. He recalls, "I went to see the man who was head of the bank"—his father's partner—"and he said to me, 'There is no room in the bank.' " The partner also told Riboud that he had "no gift for banking." Something he didn't say was that he had reserved a major position for his own son. Riboud was both depressed and relieved—depressed because his future was blank, and relieved because he would not have to become a Lyons banker. Unsure of what he wanted to do, he went to Paris to have an interview for a job in industry, and while he was there he also went to see André Istel, who had been a banking partner of Maurice Schlumberger. Riboud knew both men, since they had been friends of Camille Riboud. Istel, a French Jew, had fled to the United States during the war, and now he planned to open a New York banking office, to be called André Istel & Company. Among Istel's clients was the oilfield-service company Schlumberger. Istel and Riboud had dinner at the Hôtel Crillon, on the Place de la Concorde, and then walked along the Seine, talking, Riboud recalls, about de Gaulle, the war, the United States, economic policies, and Camille Riboud but not about the investment-banking business.

Two days later, Istel phoned Riboud's hotel to arrange an interview, and when they met again, Istel said, "I'm opening an office in New York, and I want you to come work for me."

"You're out of your mind, Monsieur Istel," Riboud recalls saying. "I can't speak a word of English. Second, I've never worked. What could I do for you?"

Istel replied, "If I had Napoleon at my disposal, I wouldn't be asking you. But I don't have Napoleon, so it's my problem, not your problem."

Two months later, in September of 1946, Riboud opened Istel's New York office, working at a salary of two hundred dollars a month. "It was another planet," he says. "Europeans had absolutely nothing. I took all my belongings to America, and I remember that they were one pair of shoes and two shirts. That's all I had— that was everything." For a year, Riboud rented a furnished room on the East Side, and then, his salary having risen, he moved into a $125-a-month apartment on Sixty-third Street between Madison and Fifth avenues. A number of art galleries were nearby, as was the Museum of Modern Art, which he particularly enjoyed. Again, as at Buchenwald, Riboud quickly learned the language being spoken around him. At the suggestion of friends in France, he got in touch with Cartier-Bresson, who at the time was being honored with his first one-man photography exhibit, at the Museum of Modern Art, and the two became lifelong friends. Riboud also met and dated Cartier-Bresson's sister, Nicole, a passionate leftist, who wrote poetry and studied psychology. They attended meetings at Cartier-Bresson's apartment, under the Manhattan side of the Queensborough Bridge; protested against Dutch colonialism in Indonesia and French colonialism in Indochina; and worked for a variety of causes. Through Cartier-Bresson, Riboud met members of the art and literary worlds, including Charles Olson, who was then living in Washington, D.C.

Olson and his wife, Constance, became special friends of Riboud's. Every two or three months, Riboud took the train to Washington to spend a weekend with them. The three would stay up talking until dawn, sleep until midafternoon, talk until dawn. Unlike Riboud, Olson came from a working-class background; his father was a mailman and a union organizer in Massachusetts. Riboud read Mao Zedong's writings aloud in French to Olson, who used several of Mao's lines in his 1949 poem "The Kingfishers," and who wrote enthusiastically of Central America's "Communist future." Olson, who was something of a mystic, taught English at Black Mountain College, in North Carolina, and was considered a leading avant-garde figure of his day. His devoted students included John Cage, Robert Rauschenberg, and Merce Cunningham.

As a young man, Riboud had become accustomed to meeting his father's literary friends, and he had read the classics; he had always cared about art and about politics; and now he shared the passions and interests of his new friends in the New York literary and artistic community. He often accompanied Langston Hughes on Sunday walks through Harlem, stopping to listen to some jazz or to the rhythmic words of preachers. He supported Charles Olson in his war with traditional forms and in his quest for new ones. He believed that Cartier-Bresson and Robert Capa, two of the founders of Magnum Photos, were artistic pioneers. He sided with Rauschenberg and others who were accused of exhibitionism, of trying to shock for the sake of shock. He spoke the language of these artists. "Like all intellectuals, Riboud has an understanding of shortcuts," Saul Steinberg has observed. "He understands paradox, and comparison that avoids lengthy explanation."

Riboud did well at the bank. He came to know some conservative businessmen and formed friendships with several—notably Garrard Winston, an attorney whose bloodline stretched back to the early days of the American republic. But investment banking did not inspire Riboud the way politics did. His was a generation that had been dominated from its early years by political questions: by Fascism, the Spanish Civil War, Hitler, the Second World War, the Holocaust, the United Nations, and colonialism; and now by Senator Joseph McCarthy. "We had to choose," Riboud says. Enemies were unambiguous. Some of those who had been aligned with him against Hitler now devoted their energies to opposing Stalin. Stalin, they argued, was another Hitler, with his own concentration camps, his own imperialistic designs on Eastern Europe. In this postwar split of the left, Riboud decried the self-proclaimed realists. He wanted the left to remain united, to remain focused on traditional enemies, to help prevent the Cold War. When Riboud thought of Communists, he thought not of a Stalin gulag but of Buchenwald, populated in part by Communists, "who had convictions and integrity," and who had saved his life. At that point, nobody, he has said, "could make me believe that the French Communists were bad."

When Alger Hiss, whom Riboud knew, was successfully prosecuted by the federal government and later attacked by McCarthy, Riboud supported Hiss, opposing those who believed that Hiss was a Soviet spy. He

saw the Hiss case as a modern-day version of the Drey-
fus case. He wasn't sure—still isn't, he says—whether
Hiss was innocent or guilty, and he felt that in a way
it didn't matter. He could excuse transgressions on the
part of Hiss, for he was certain that the forces of oppres-
sion, of militarism, of narrow nationalism were mobilized on the other side. As he had when he joined the
Resistance, he felt that he had to choose. It was a matter
of "us" against "them." Today, Riboud sees the Hiss
case as "the beginning of something that was fairly
important, part of American history that is resurrected
now with Mr. Reagan, which is the peace problem, the
McCarthy problem, witch-hunts—really, the problem
of freedom in America." Saul Steinberg says of that
time, "Whenever we sat down in a group of people, we
looked around to see who would join us on the barri-
cades."

In the spring of 1947, Riboud went to a party for
Cartier-Bresson given by the editor of *Harper's Bazaar*,
and there he met Krishna Roy. She was one of "three
absolutely adorable, beautiful young Indian girls"—his
words—who were visiting from Wellesley College, where
they were studying philosophy. Krishna Roy was born
in Dacca on October 12, 1926, and, like Riboud, she
had grown up comfortably. Her father, Rajendra Roy,
had been director of public health in East Bengal, and
the family of her mother, Ena Tagore, included the poet
Rabindranath Tagore and a revolutionary leader, Soumyendranath Tagore. Rajendra Roy died when Krishna
was ten, and she grew up in the city of Calcutta under
the tutelage of her uncle Soumyendranath, who had a
lasting influence on her. "My uncle, whom I had a
passion for, was a revolutionary Marxist, and his Marx-
ism was very different from the Communism we know
now," recalls Krishna Riboud, a short woman with dark
skin and straight black hair. Full of idealistic fervor,
her uncle visited the Soviet Union between 1927 and
1929; he became a friend of Nikolai Bukharin, the Rus-

sian Communist theoretician, and slowly became horrified by Stalin's ruthless consolidation of power. After
returning home, he, like Gandhi and Jawaharlal Nehru,
was repeatedly arrested by the British colonial administration for revolutionary activities. Krishna vividly
remembers a time at the Calcutta railway station when
she saw her uncle manacled by British police and carted
off on a train.

A well-placed friend helped to obtain the release of
her uncle on that occasion, and, later, helped get Krishna
into Wellesley. The friend was Spencer Kellogg, Jr.,
scion of a wealthy family, who had met Krishna's family when his daughter Lois became ill on a visit to India
and was treated by Krishna's father. When Kellogg returned to the United States, he wrote to Krishna's mother
to suggest that Krishna be allowed to enroll at Wellesley. Nehru's sister, Vijaya Lakshmi Pandit, who later
became president of the United National General Assembly, had sent her daughters there, so Ena Tagore
Roy did not immediately dismiss the suggestion. Then
Lois Kellogg wrote to say that she would be Krishna's
guardian, and that Krishna could spend winter vacations with her at the Kelloggs' home in Scottsdale, Arizona, and weekends at their home in Connecticut. After
a time, Mrs. Roy consented. In 1945, Krishna Roy went
to Wellesley. She was not just another foreign student.
She came with letters of introduction from John Dewey
and Albert Einstein, both of whom knew her uncle the
poet and her uncle the revolutionary. She remembers
visiting John Dewey, who cautioned her not to study
Western philosophy. She remembers driving to Princeton on a rainy day to meet Einstein. "I walked into this
small house, and he asked, 'How is your uncle?' " she
says. "He was so sweet. He took me up to a small ver-
anda and made some tea. He said to his daughter, 'She's
the niece of that wonderful Communist, Tagore.' Then
he played the violin for me."

The first time Krishna Roy and Jean Riboud spoke at

any length, they, too, spoke of her uncle the revolutionary. She had seen Riboud at the Cartier-Bresson gathering but had paid no heed to him—he had made "no impression whatsoever," she recalls. After that first meeting, however, he invited her for a walk, and in the course of it he asked about her uncles, her country, her philosophy studies. They argued, he remembers, about modern art, which they both admired. They began to see each other regularly. Two years later, Riboud told her, "If we are going to keep on seeing each other, we must take a trip together around the country." She agreed, and Jean invited his sister Françoise, to whom he was still very close, to join them. It was the summer of 1949, and they traveled by car to Seattle and the Pacific, to Arizona, and across the country to the Olsons' house at Black Mountain College.

In 1949, Krishna and Jean decided to get married, though they knew that Ena Tagore Roy wanted her daughter to marry an Indian national, and that Hélène Riboud wanted her son to marry a Catholic. With encouragement from Françoise, they decided to write to their mothers and announce their intention, but not to wait for replies. On October 1, 1949, Krishna and Jean were married by a priest at the Kelloggs' house in Connecticut. Françoise was matron of honor, and Krishna was attended by her close friend Rita Pandit. The wedding party included Charles Olson, A. J. Liebling, Anne Schlumberger Doll and her husband, Henri, and other members of the Schlumberger family, who were principal clients of André Istel & Company.

The Schlumberger family had been watching Jean Riboud. Glowing reports arrived from André Istel and Maurice Schlumberger. The Schlumbergers had come to know Riboud directly, because a third of the investment bank's financial-advisory business was with their company or with the family itself. Riboud was invited to family dinners, and impressed other guests with his knowledge of politics, art, and literature. One day, Marcel Schlumberger arrived at the house of his niece Anne, in Ridgefield, Connecticut. She recalls that he seemed depressed. Schlumberger had always been a family company, and Mr. Marcel, as he was called, usually hired its engineers himself. But the company was growing rapidly—it now had offices not only in Paris but also in Ridgefield and Houston—and Marcel worried that it was becoming too successful, too bureaucratized, and would lose its sense of intimacy and fall into the hands of men without character. Anne listened to Marcel's lament, and after a while the talk turned to Jean Riboud. "You see him now and then," he said. "What do you think of this lad?"

In *The Schlumberger Adventure*, a family memoir published in the United States in January of 1983, Anne (who, divorced from Henri Doll, had become Anne Gruner Schlumberger) writes that she replied, "I think he has a heart—a feeling for humanity, I guess I want to say. That's rare enough in someone committed to high finance. If you're thinking of taking him on, I'll be surprised if he disappoints you."

"Oh, I find him *sympathique*," Marcel said. "We'll see." He paused, then added, "I wouldn't know how to use him. Finance is not our business, and I don't believe in it."

Marcel arranged to have lunch with Riboud in Paris in July of 1950. Jean and Krishna had had a son, Christophe, that year, and had talked often of starting a new life in France. Riboud felt unfulfilled as an investment banker. He was restless in America, and was concerned that he was losing touch with France. Moreover, he had never been to India; he wanted to go there, and then settle in Paris and maybe open a bookstore. Earlier that year, he had notified André Istel that he planned to leave the banking business and go to India for six months. Now, when Marcel learned of these plans, he offered Riboud an undefined position with Schlumberger. "I haven't the foggiest idea what you'll do," he said at lunch. He offered to pay Riboud $500 a month—$2500 a month less than he was then making. He proposed to send him to Houston as an assistant to his son, Pierre, but Riboud, because of his Indian-born wife, made it clear he would not live in the South. Still, he was intrigued by Schlumberger and by the sense of adventure that the oil business promised. He agreed to go to work for the company, but on two conditions: he must first visit India, and he must work at Schlumberger's Paris office. Marcel accepted his terms.

The Ribouds sailed for France in January of 1951, and stayed at the Paris flat of Dominique and Jean de Ménil for a week, during which Hélène Riboud came to visit. Then Krishna, Jean, and Christophe embarked on a two-day plane trip to Calcutta, where Riboud met the Tagore and Roy families, and was extensively exposed to Eastern culture and the Hindu faith. Awestruck, he traveled throughout the country, asking questions, admiring the art and the traditions. He has visited India every year but one for the past three decades.

Upon returning to France, in May of 1951, Riboud went to work at Schlumberger. He worked on finances, on merging what had become four independent Schlumberger companies into one, but mostly he listened. "For the first year, I really did nothing except listen to Marcel," he says. "Marcel used him as a gadfly," says Paul Lepercq, who is also from Lyons and was recruited by Riboud as his replacement at the New York bank; today Lepercq is the second-longest-serving member of the Schlumberger board of directors. Riboud watched Marcel—the "adapter," as Paul Schlumberger called him—spend hours asking penetrating questions, or sit through meetings without saying a word, his eyes unreadable under thick eyebrows, his expression blank. Marcel focused on personnel decisions, which, he told Riboud, were the most important decisions an executive had to make. Even though Marcel was approaching seventy, he would cross the ocean to attend meetings of engineers and managers. William Gillingham, a British-born engineer who had been hired by Marcel in 1934 and had become the head of Schlumberger's oil-field-service operations, recalls saying, "Mr. Marcel, you must enjoy coming over here and hearing these technical papers," and that Marcel glared at him and said, "Mr. Gillingham, I don't come here to hear these papers. I can read them in my office. I come here to see what kind of people are running my company."

Riboud learned that nothing seemed to please Marcel. Although Marcel is said never to have raised his voice, he was hardly a diplomat. Jérôme Seydoux, the son of Marcel's daughter, Geneviève, recalls, "He disliked anything that was not well done." The old man often spent weekends at their country home in Cormeilles, outside Paris. "He could be quite rude," Seydoux says. "If a meal was not good, he would say to us, 'It's not good'—and wouldn't eat it. One sentence or one word was enough. He gave us a sense that you have to do quality work. If things were perfect, he'd say, 'C'est bien'—but that's all." Marcel disliked frills. If an employee bought an expensive carpet or piece of furniture for his office, Marcel would bark a few gruff monosyllables at him. He would complain if there were too many words in a telegram. He lived for the company. Monday mornings, Marcel arrived at the office and asked his employees what new thoughts about Schlumberger they had had over the weekend. If they had had shrewd insights or had done outstanding work, he offered no compliments. "When he was really friends with you, he offered you a cigarette," says Claude Baks, who joined Schlumberger as an engineer in 1946. He later became one of Riboud's principal advisers, and remembers Mr. Marcel with great affection.

Despite his flaws, Marcel communicated to Riboud his almost religious devotion to Schlumberger. As with other corporate pioneers—Thomas J. Watson, of IBM, A. P. Giannini, of the Bank of America, Henry Ford— this devotion became a legend. Riboud speaks of an incident that took place in 1940, when the Germans had invaded Belgium and were poised to overwhelm France. Erle P. Halliburton, the head of the Halliburton Oil Well Cementing Company, which was Schlumberger's chief oilfield-service rival, paid a visit to Marcel. "Everybody knew that France was going to be defeated, that Paris would be totally cut off from Houston, and that Houston wouldn't survive by itself, without Paris," Riboud says. Halliburton offered to buy Schlumberger for $10 million. Marcel made no reply but slowly rose from his chair, and beckoned Halliburton to follow him. They walked silently to the elevator, where Marcel thanked his visitor and said goodbye. Another executive might have hesitated, Riboud says. Why didn't Marcel? "Because there are some questions you never discuss," he says. "If somebody were to come and ask you to sell your wife, you wouldn't hesitate to say no, would you?" Riboud draws a lesson from this tale: Marcel Schlumberger was never swayed by passing storms, because he remained anchored to a set of beliefs. "The first was, Think for yourself," Riboud says. "Whatever is happening at the moment, try to think for yourself."

In the summer of 1953, at the age of sixty-nine, Marcel died of heart failure. In a eulogy, Jean de Ménil said, "He had known for several weeks that he had not much time left to live. He never alluded to it. With those who entered his office, he would discuss, listen, and advise as usual. To his wife, a few days before his death, he said, 'My motor is stalling.' Then, on August 20, in the late morning, he retired to his room without a complaint. He died as he had lived: upright."

Although Marcel's corporate heirs shared his sense of the company's special mission, his death robbed Schlumberger of its central authority. Feuds surfaced among the branches of the Schlumberger family. No one emerged as chief executive officer to replace Marcel. Instead, the company was divided into four fiefdoms, each ruled by a family member. The technical side of the business was the domain of Henri Doll, the husband of Conrad's daughter Anne, and the engineer who in 1927 performed the first successful wireline experiment. Doll, who believed fervently in technology, pushed the company to apportion a larger share of its profits for his research activities. Science was Doll's forte, his love. He fled France in 1940 and lent his skills to the Allied cause. Doll supported his small company, Electro-Mechanical Research—which he started in Houston and moved to Ridgefield, Connecticut, after the war—with defense contracts. There he invented a device to detect land mines, and helped perfect rocketry-guidance systems. When the war ended, Schlumberger bought this company, and under Doll's direction the Ridgefield lab produced the first induction log, a device using electromagnetic waves to measure resistivity, which increased Schlumberger's lead in the wireline business. William Gillingham has estimated that when Doll retired, in 1967, 40 percent of Schlumberger's revenues sprang from his inventions. But Doll was a scientist, not a corporate manager; although he ranked first in seniority when Marcel died, he chose not to assume the leadership of the company.

Pierre Schlumberger, the only son of Marcel—and the only son of either founder—ruled the most profitable division: Schlumberger's North American wireline operations. Schlumberger came out of the war a weakened company, with its executives scattered. In 1946, Pierre set up an organization in Houston that would keep pace with the growing American oil market. Like his father, Pierre was a man of simple convictions. With his father gone, he came to believe that if Schlumberger was to grow it had to become a public company rather than remaining a family one, and that it had to make its financial operations more professional—to codify a set of rules rather than follow the whims of one man. Pierre had ambitious plans, but other family members resisted them.

A third sector—Schlumberger's wireline operations in South America and the Middle East—was run from Houston by Jean de Ménil, the husband of Conrad's daughter Dominique. For eight years after his marriage, de Ménil, a Paris banker, resisted Marcel's importunings to join the company, but in 1939 he did, and became responsible for Schlumberger's financial structure. During the war, de Ménil successfully schemed with Marcel to free the company from potential Nazi control by shifting its base of operations from France to Trinidad. And after the war de Ménil played a large part in making Schlumberger a truly international corporation, by requiring that all business be conducted in English and that the dollar be the common currency, as is now customary in the oil business. Like Conrad Schlumberger, de Ménil was an idealist, and lent his financial support to political and artistic movements that challenged the status quo. And, also like Conrad, he believed that Schlumberger's ability to help others find oil was a natural extension of his political beliefs. "You were bringing to human frontiers technology that helped people," says his son George de Ménil, who is an economist. "During the war, it contributed something crucial to the growth of the world economy."

Schlumberger's European operations—the fourth fiefdom—were run by Marcel's son-in-law, René Seydoux. Like de Ménil, he had intense political convictions, and he became a supporter of the French Socialist Party. During the war, he was captured by the Germans and sent to a prisoner-of-war camp. After the war, he returned to Schlumberger and was made head of its Paris office. Among those who worked for him following Marcel's death was Jean Riboud, who admired his gentle nature. Through Seydoux, Riboud came to know many Socialist Party leaders. Of the four family members, a person who knew them well says, "The others were stronger personalities in a sense, but René Seydoux was always the cement, trying to hold things together."

The cement did not adhere. For three years after Marcel Schlumberger's death, the company remained divided into four parts. Relations among the family members were amicable, professional, often affectionate. The four parts were united in their devotion to Schlumberger and its mission, but there was no central planning and coordination. Riboud and other executives disliked this arrangement, and campaigned to restructure the corporation. Finally, in 1956, a new parent company, Schlumberger Limited, was created to unify operations. Pierre Schlumberger became president; Henri Doll was elected chairman of the board. The company was incorporated on the island of Curaçao, in the Netherlands Antilles, which was then becoming one of the world's prime tax havens.

Pierre Schlumberger, in Houston, supervised the company's worldwide operations. He took the company public, selling shares on the New York Stock Exchange, and declared that family members would no longer receive preference within the company for promotion. This angered family members, who were uneasy, in Riboud's words, because they wished "to keep family control of the company"—but as profits rose discontent dissipated. In 1959, however, Pierre's wife died, and over the next eighteen months Pierre stayed at home most days. When he did come to the office, he was irritable and autocratic. He sometimes arrived at board meetings hours late. His period of grief ended when he met and quickly married a beautiful young Portuguese woman, Maria da Diniz Concerçao—known today as Sao Schlumberger—but his erratic behavior did not, for he had grown fond of café society. "Pierre was very fragile and lost his balance," observes his cousin Anne Gruner Schlumberger. By this time, Doll, de Ménil, and Seydoux were near retirement. Schlumberger executives pleaded with them, for the good of the company, to intercede. Jean Riboud was then the general manager in charge of all Schlumberger operations in Europe and the eastern hemisphere. Under Pierre's direction, he essentially ran half the empire, while the North and South American half was run by Aime Vennema, an American working in Houston. Riboud was "always Pierre's choice to succeed him," says Paul Lepercq, who was then a member of the executive committee. But there was "a big power play," he recalls, with the company's chief financial officer, Carl Neureuther, an ally of Pierre's, warring with the six other members of the executive committee. Riboud, as one of the six, stood opposite Neureuther. Yet he was somewhat ambivalent, telling associates that the situation was intolerable but adding that he cared too much for Pierre to depose him. Lepercq, as a board member and also the family banker, met with other members of the family, all of whom felt that Pierre must leave. "They took over power from him," Claude Baks recalls. "Everyone was in on it. I was in the middle of it."

Eventually, the factions came to agree on the man who should be Pierre's successor—Jean Riboud. Everyone knew Marcel Schlumberger's former assistant. The branches of the Schlumberger family disagreed about many things, but not about the value of Riboud. Everyone saw in him familiar qualities. Like Marcel, he was an asker of questions, a quiet, wise man. Like Conrad, he took an interest in his employees and in leftist politics. Like Pierre, he was a professional manager, and his very appointment would demonstrate that Schlumberger was no longer a family fiefdom. He was dignified, like de Ménil; gentle, like Seydoux; a believer in research, like Doll. He shared with them a fervent faith in Schlumberger. And he was seen, after Pierre, as Marcel's chosen heir. "I know that Marcel felt that his end

was near and that his death might precipitate an outbreak of discord that would bring down the work to
which he and his brother had given their best," Anne
Gruner Schlumberger writes in her memoir. "To take
Jean Riboud under his wing, form him in his school,
and bequeath to him the stamp of his authority was, to
his thinking, the way to avoid the worst."

In early May of 1965, the family asked Riboud to
replace Pierre Schlumberger. Riboud says that he immediately resigned, declaring, "I will not replace Pierre,
because I owe too much friendship to him. The only
decent thing for me to do is to resign." The family
prevailed on Pierre to resign first, and then asked Riboud to become president and chief executive officer
of Schlumberger. He did so on May 13, 1965.

3

THE PATH TO THE TOP

For eighteen years, Riboud has ruled Schlumberger, in the words of one company executive, "like an absolutely constitutional monarch." Felix Rohatyn says, "He is the absolute, unquestioned boss in the company. His authority is as absolute as that of any chief executive I've seen." When Riboud speaks of Schlumberger, he often does so in the first person singular. Explaining, for example, Schlumberger's 1979 acquisition of the Fairchild Camera & Instrument Corporation, he says, "It seemed to me . . ." Although he is not a Schlumberger, his authority within the family is comparable to that of Conrad or Marcel. "He has the unanimity of the family behind him," according to Dominique de Ménil, who is now seventy-five and is a close friend of Riboud's. Since the Schlumberger family owns about a fourth of the company's stock, the support of the family is significant. Still, because Schlumberger has generated consistently higher profits under his reign, because he has succeeded in completing the transformation of a family enterprise into a public company, because he is acclaimed on Wall Street, and because he has at times ruthlessly asserted his authority, Riboud has assured his independence.

The only overt challenge to Riboud's reign has come from Jérôme Seydoux. From the time Jérôme was a little boy, Marcel Schlumberger had urged his grandson to become an engineer. Jérôme heeded the advice and, in 1959, received a degree in electrical engineering from L'École Nationale Supérieure d'Électronique, d'Électrotechnique et d'Hydraulique, in Toulouse. But by then Marcel was dead, and Jérôme's uncle Pierre, determined to make Schlumberger a public company, discouraged him from joining it until he had proved his worth elsewhere. "To some extent, it was a shock to me," Seydoux recalls. "I had been educated to work for Schlumberger." Instead, he went to work for the family's investment-banking firm, Istel, Lepercq & Co., the successor to André Istel's firm. In the early 1960s, Jérôme Seydoux worked under Paul Lepercq in New York; then, in 1963, having climbed rapidly, he returned to Paris, where he became a partner. He had more than the right name; he also had talent. He is a handsome man with pale-blue eyes and blondish hair that falls onto his forehead, and even today, at the age of forty-eight, he has a boyish appearance. By the end of the sixties, he had caught the attention of Riboud. In 1969, Jérôme's father, René, retired from the board of directors, and Riboud invited Jérôme to join it. He hailed the younger Seydoux as one of the brightest men of his generation, valued his advice, and took him into his counsel, as Marcel Schlumberger had done with Riboud.

In 1969, while Seydoux was vacationing in the South of France, Riboud phoned and asked to meet him on a matter of urgency. Seydoux still remembers the date of the meeting—the first day of May. Riboud offered Seydoux a job with Schlumberger. Some months later, Schlumberger acquired the Compagnie des Compteurs, a French manufacturer of electric meters and other instruments, and Riboud offered Seydoux the job of president. The company had been losing money, but Riboud believed that it could become profitable. Riboud remembers telling Seydoux that if he succeeded with the new acquisition he would have "a big future." Seydoux remembers Riboud's saying that he would become president of Schlumberger. In any case, Seydoux did succeed, transforming the company into a profitable operation that is now known as Measurement & Control–Europe. Six years later, in September of 1975, Riboud appointed Seydoux president of Schlumberger, retaining the positions of chief executive officer and chairman of the board. Seydoux remained president for just eighteen weeks. His memory of his tenure remains vivid. Now president of Chargeurs SA, a major Paris transportation company, Seydoux recently told a visitor to his office, "I always worked very well with Riboud. We talked easily and communicated well. Yet a few days after I became president he wasn't happy. It lasted four and one-half months, but I really think it lasted only a week. Very soon after I became president, we stopped communicating."

In the opinion of people who knew him then, Seydoux began acting as if he were the chief executive— as if the family dynasty had been restored. When he moved into his new office, one of his first acts was to hang on the wall over his desk a picture of his grandfather Marcel Schlumberger. Riboud thought that Seydoux was acting like someone who believed that his station was inherited, and not earned. Riboud's unease was intensified by complaints from executives who had been instructed to report to Seydoux. Jérôme was too officious, too brusque, they protested. William Gillingham says that Jérôme lacked "the human touch." Some executives were doubtless unhappy that they no longer reported directly to Riboud, and Riboud himself was unhappy, because he had discovered that at the age of fifty-five he did not want to step aside.

Riboud, having decided to dismiss Seydoux, acted with military precision: he met with or telephoned every other member of the board—there were sixteen members—and said that there was not room for two corporate heads at Schlumberger and that he planned to dismiss Seydoux. With the board's approval, he visited and won the concurrence of five of the six branches of the Schlumberger family. And then, one winter morning, he summoned Seydoux to his New York apartment, at the Carlton House, on Madison Avenue. In his soft, polite way, Riboud said that he was unhappy with the current arrangement and asked Seydoux to leave. "It was not a pleasant conversation, but it was not harsh," Seydoux recalls. They talked for an hour, and then walked to the corporate offices on Park Avenue, where Seydoux asked his secretary to get him a reservation on the first plane to Paris. He left an hour later, never to return. "I didn't like it, but I understood that he was the boss," Seydoux remarks, adding that he is not bitter about the experience and that he and Riboud occasionally see each other socially.

Riboud, as he demonstrated with Seydoux, is not timid about firing people. "Jean has less difficulty facing up to tough personal decisions than any other executive I know. Most executives dread it," Felix Rohatyn says. Carl Buchholz, an American who started as an engineer, was once vice-president of personnel, and who is now president of The Analysts, says, "One of my predecessors sat outside Riboud's office all day, and Riboud wouldn't talk to him. If someone was blowing hot air in my office, I'd say, 'Get the hell out of here!' If you're blowing hot air around Riboud, he'll smile and put his arm around you and walk you to the door and make you feel good—and you'll never get in there again."

A man who sulks after losing at golf or at gin rummy—something that Riboud does—is capable of holding grudges. "When something goes wrong, it's finished," says Jeannine Bourhis, Riboud's secretary in Paris for the past thirteen years. "Jérôme Seydoux was family. He liked Jérôme very much, too. And all of a sudden—*phiff!*" In 1971, without receiving permission, Jean-Jacques Servan-Schreiber, a longtime friend and ally on the French left, announced to the press that Riboud was a political supporter. Riboud almost immediately sold all his shares in *L'Express*, Servan-Schreiber's magazine, and for ten years refused to speak to him. In 1966, Riboud was enraged when Magnum Photos, which, by Riboud's estimate, had received about a million dollars in business from his company (a Magnum official says that at most they received $50,000 in business from Schlumberger), sued Schlumberger for losing some negatives. His brother Marc was then a member of Magnum's board, which further enraged Jean. Riboud issued an order never to give Magnum another piece of business, though he had been one of the company's early and enthusiastic supporters. He does not talk about these grudges, seems not to stew over them. In a sense, they have become impersonal. Riboud simply closes the book, treats family or friends as if they were dead. "He's like an elephant," says Henri Cartier-Bresson. "He never forgets."

"Riboud handles personnel matters as if no personalities were involved," says Benno Schmidt, who is a managing partner of J. H. Whitney & Company and was a member of Schlumberger's board from 1973 to 1982. "If he considers you the wrong man, he'll remove you in five seconds. He's invariably generous as far as the personal welfare of the person is concerned, but he feels no obligation to keep people in jobs they're not doing. It's matter-of-fact." Several months after making those remarks, Schmidt himself felt the cold side of Riboud. Riboud visited Schmidt in his office, on Fifth Avenue, and told him that after prolonged deliberation he had decided that Schmidt and three other board members should retire. (Board members who were not also employees of the company received $24,000 annually for their services and $9,000 more if they served on the executive committee, the audit committee, or the finance committee.) Riboud did not ask whether Schmidt, a sometime golfing partner and a member of the Schlumberger executive committee, wanted to step aside. He simply told Schmidt politely that he must go. Riboud explained that he was reimposing a mandatory retirement age of sixty-eight for board members in order to ease a particular individual off the board and also to inject "new blood" into the corporate leadership. Riboud said that he saw no way to avoid applying this rule to his friend Schmidt. Schmidt had risen from poverty in Abilene, Texas, to become editor in chief of the *University of Texas Law Review*, a professor of law at Harvard, an Army officer during the Second World War, a managing partner of J. H. Whitney, and an intimate of presidents and senators. His pride was wounded, but he did not complain. Riboud, knowing his associate, was prepared to assuage the hurt. He said he would like Don E. Ackerman, one of Schmidt's protégés at J. H. Whitney, to take his seat on the board, and he invited Schmidt to attend subsequent board and executive-committee sessions, including the summer board meeting in Paris.

At the quarterly gathering of the board in New York on February 18, 1982, Riboud gave Schmidt and the other deposed board members an elaborate sendoff. Speaking from handwritten notes, he said that reimposing the mandatory retirement age was "one of the tougher decisions of my professional life." He then paid tribute to each retiring board member. The "forcefulness of his personality," he said, gave Benno Schmidt "a unique position on our board." The "financial background" and "the gentleness, the charm of his personality" made Ellmore C. (Pat) Patterson, former chairman of the Morgan Guaranty Trust Company, "the best member of the finance committee." Jacques de Fouchier, chairman of the Compagnie Financière de Paris et des Pays-Bas (Paribas), which is one of the largest banks in France, brought to the board "simplicity" and "steadfastness" and "judgment . . . unsurpassed in my business experience." Finally, he said of Françoise Primat, a daughter of Marcel Schlumberger and the owner of the largest block of Schlumberger stock (4 percent), that although she "did not talk very much" and had missed a score of meetings since joining the board, in 1965, "I have not known a more loyal, friendly, active supporter."

Riboud understood that the moment called for diplomacy, but he also felt that the time had come to bring fresh thinking to the board and to begin preparing for an eventual successor. He had harmonious relations with all four of the deposed board members, but the one he was genuinely sorry to lose was de Fouchier. "I can't retire Pat and Schmidt at sixty-nine and not retire de Fouchier at seventy-one," he said. Those close to Riboud say that he felt Schmidt had become too set in his ways, too predictable, and that there was also some concern that he was pushing to become chairman of the board—a position from which he might influence the choice of Riboud's successor. When Patterson retired as chairman of Morgan Guaranty several years before, he weakened his claim to represent what Riboud called "the Eastern financial establishment." Riboud wanted such a representative to head the company's audit committee, of which Patterson was also a member. To replace Patterson, Riboud sought the current chairman of the bank, Lewis T. Preston—a move that softened the jolt to Patterson. However, Riboud asked Preston to resign from the board of General Electric before joining Schlumberger's board. Preston said no, because his rival Walter Wriston, the chairman of Citibank, was also on the GE board. On the other hand, Preston did not wish to relinquish his bank's investment in Schlumberger. (In 1981, the Morgan Guaranty

Trust Company made loans of nearly $214 million to Schlumberger, and received interest payments of $25 million and fees of $283,000.) Preston suggested another Morgan executive as a replacement for Patterson. Having anticipated this countermove, Riboud not only rejected it but had already asked Richard Shinn, then the chairman and chief executive officer of the Metropolitan Life Insurance Company, to serve. "I took a little gamble by talking to him before I talked to Preston," Riboud admits. Françoise Primat was deposed for several reasons. Not only had she missed many meetings but she wished to leave and hoped to have her son, Didier Primat, who was then thirty-eight years old, take her place—a hope that Riboud did not share. Riboud saw her prospective vacancy as an opportunity to engage in some family fence-mending. To replace Françoise Primat, he selected Jérôme Seydoux's younger brother Nicolas, a Paris businessman, who was then forty-two. Before making the commitment, however, he warned Nicolas Seydoux that his "obligation was to the stockholders, not the family."

Like a politician who balances a ticket, Riboud was left with a board whose outside directors balanced several of what he calls his "constituencies." The Schlumberger family is represented by Nicolas Seydoux; by George de Ménil, forty-two, a son of Dominique and Jean; and by Pierre Marcel Schlumberger, forty, a Houston attorney, who is a son of Pierre. The American financial establishment is represented by Shinn, sixty-five; the French business community is represented by Renault's chairman, Bernard Hanon, fifty-one, who replaced de Fouchier; Houston's establishment is represented by George H. Jewell, sixty-one, a law partner in the influential firm of Baker & Botts, which performs legal work for Schlumberger; Wall Street is represented by Felix Rohatyn, fifty-five, a general partner in Lazard Freres & Company, which received $1,565,949 in fees for handling Schlumberger's acquisitions in 1981; and access to the intellectual and technological community is provided by Jerome B. Wiesner, sixty-eight, the former science adviser to President John F. Kennedy and currently the president emeritus of the Massachusetts Institute of Technology.

Riboud's ability to control the membership of the board is but one example of his absolute command of Schlumberger. Over the years, he has removed from the company four family members: Marcel Schlumberger's only son, Pierre; Marcel's daughter Françoise Primat; Marcel's grandson Jérôme Seydoux, who was also the son of Riboud's former boss; and, in 1958, Eric Boissonas, who had married Conrad Schlumberger's youngest daughter, Sylvie, and was a vice-president of research. (Boissonas was dismissed because Pierre Schlumberger, supported by Riboud, had business differences with him.) In each case, Riboud felt that for the good of the company he had to ignore personal sentiment. Jerome Wiesner makes a distinction between being tough and being mean: "Tough has a connotation of *mean* to me. I don't think there's a mean side to him . . . He can separate his human feelings and what he feels is necessary for the company. Any successful chief officer must. The worst failing of any executive is the inability to separate his personal regard for the people from his judgment of what is necessary for the welfare of the company."

Whatever personal pain Riboud feels is soothed by the conviction that loyalty to the company outweighs personal loyalties. He believes that he is simply doing his duty. "If you want to be St. Francis of Assisi, you should not head a public company," he says.

4

A MANAGERIAL PHILOSOPHY

The man, his style of management—and the nature of the company he manages—can be gleaned by following Jean Riboud on one of his frequent field trips, this one to Schlumberger's North American Wireline operations in Texas, the most profitable of their three worldwide wireline divisions. It is commonly assumed that the heart of the oil business pumps in the Middle East. That is not so. At the beginning of 1982, 70 percent of the world's active oil-drilling rigs outside of the Soviet bloc were in the United States and Canada. Because of the current oil glut, the number of active drilling rigs in North America fell from 4700 in January of 1982 to 1990 in March of 1983, but that was still more than the 1200 active rigs operating in the rest of the non-Communist world. The United States produces more barrels of oil daily (about 8.6 million) than Saudi Arabia (about 4.6 million). And Schlumberger's Wireline division generates 45 percent of the corporation's revenues and an estimated 70 percent of its net profits. It is therefore not surprising that this division occupies much of Riboud's time.

On a recent Friday afternoon, Riboud, accompanied by André Misk, a former field engineer who is a vice-president and the director of comunications, went to Teterboro Airport, in New Jersey, and boarded one of six jet airplanes belonging to the company for a flight to Houston. In Houston, Riboud stayed at the home of Aime Vennema, who rose from field engineer to chairman of the executive committee before he retired, and who shares Riboud's love of gin rummy, golf, and modern art. Friday evening was set aside for a quiet dinner with Vennema and his wife, Kay. Saturday was devoted to golf with Vennema and attorney George Jewell. Saturday evening, wearing a V-neck sweater pulled over a beige turtleneck, Riboud met Dominique de Ménil on the Rice University campus, where they viewed an Yves Klein art exhibit that Mrs. de Ménil, a patron of modern art, had helped lure to the Rice Museum. Riboud, who often disparages business fads and social fashions, does have a weakness for what he considers "new thinking," whether it is in art or politics. He was much taken with the monochrome canvases of Klein, a French artist who died of a heart attack at the age of thirty-four, and who was known for inviting the press to watch him jump from buildings to help prove that air was art, and for getting nude models to bathe in paint and roll on his canvases. Challenged about the value of Klein's art, Riboud says, "Who are we to know what will be important fifty years from now? People have dismissed Cubism and surrealism and modern art. That is the reaction people have to all innovation."

After seeing the exhibit, Riboud had dinner at Dominique de Ménil's house—the first house ever designed by the architect Philip Johnson. Surrounded by 17th-century Venetian furniture, which Riboud recognized, and by the works of such artists as Max Ernst, Jasper Johns, Robert Rauschenberg, and Giorgio de Chirico, they discussed, among other things, former Secretary of State Henry Kissinger, for whom Riboud has little respect. Riboud's animosity toward Kissinger stems in part from Kissinger's views on foreign policy—what Riboud refers to as Kissinger's contempt for Western European opinion and for the Third World. He told Mrs. de Ménil that Kissinger was too cynical, too disdainful of European opinion, had been too preoccupied with proving to President Richard Nixon that he was free of parochial loyalties to his native Europe. Riboud's attitude toward Kissinger is also based, in part, on a personal encounter in 1980. Riboud was spending a summer weekend at Southampton with Felix Rohatyn and his wife, Elizabeth. Together, they watched the televised Wimbledon final match between Björn Borg, of Sweden, and John McEnroe, of the United States. That evening, they had cocktails with William Paley, then chairman of CBS, and Kissinger, who happened to be staying with Paley, and at one point the talk turned to the Wimbledon final. According to Riboud and another guest, Kissinger said, "I've met many people in my life, but the two people I cannot stand in the world are the Swedes and the Indians."

After a clumsy silence, Rohatyn interjected, "Henry, you know that Jean is married to an Indian woman?"

After another silence, Kissinger asked solicitously, "Where is your wife from in India?"

Riboud does not recall his response, but he does recall that this confirmed his worst suspicions about Kissinger's hostility toward Europe and the Third World. Kissinger says that he has "no recollection" of using such stereotypes, but adds, "It's possible in my life that I've said unfriendly things about Swedes or Indians in the context of their self-righteousness."

The next day in Houston Riboud spent playing golf, and then he had drinks with Pierre Marcel Schlumberger and dinner at the Vennemas' with seven past or present Schlumberger executives and their wives, charming them, as he always does, by remembering their children's names, by asking them questions.

On Monday morning at nine, Riboud went to the office of Ian Strecker, who has been in charge of Schlumberger's wireline, engineering, and manufacturing operations in North America since the beginning of 1982. Strecker is a burly, gregarious man of forty-three whose normal work outfit consists of cowboy boots, an open-necked sports shirt, and slacks. He joined Schlumberger twenty-one years ago in England, where he was born, and has since held twenty jobs in eighteen different locations. Part of Riboud's purpose in meeting with Strecker was to get a feel for him and other employees in order to gauge, in Marcel Schlumberger's words, "What kind of people are running *my* company." One of Riboud's preoccupations is that Schlumberger will lose its drive as a company and grow complacent—a concern he had discussed on the plane to Houston. "Any business, any society has a built-in force to be conservative," he said. "The whole nature of human society is to be conservative. If you want to innovate, to change an enterprise or a society, it takes people willing to do what's not expected. The basic vision I have, and what I'm trying to do at Schlumberger, is no different from what I think should be done in French or American society." In other words, sow doubt. Rotate people. Don't measure just the profits in a given division—measure the man in charge, too, and his enthusiasm for change.

Strecker's predecessor, Roy Shourd, learned at first hand just what Riboud means. Shourd headed the North American Wireline division from 1977 through 1981, and in those years its profits rose an average of 30 percent annually. But Riboud worried that Shourd was growing complacent with success, that he was surrounding himself with an inbred group of executives and becoming too clubby with the Houston oil establishment, so late in 1981 he suddenly shifted Shourd to New York and a staff job. (Typically, one year later, in another surprising move, Riboud elevated Shourd to the position of executive vice-president for drilling and production services. Riboud was satisfied that Shourd's year in exile had reignited his competitive spirit.)

This visit to Houston allowed Riboud to take the measure of Strecker, whom he did not know well. Strecker's office is in a three-story red brick building overlooking Houston's Gulf Freeway. Strecker and Riboud sat down at an oval cherrywood conference table, and then Riboud, who had arrived with no reports or notes, silently inspected his fingernails, formed his long fingers into a steeple, on which he rested his chin, and began the meeting. He asked, solicitously, how Strecker's wife, Elaine, had adjusted to Houston, how their two sons, who had remained in school in England, were getting on, how the Streckers had enjoyed a recent visit to England. Before long, the meeting got around to specific employees. Riboud made detailed comments on them, giving not only his impression of their abilities but also his impression of how well their abilities were matched to their jobs. He emphasized that final judgments on all employees were Strecker's to make. After Riboud had finished with the personnel matters, he asked Strecker if he had been spending much time in the field—among the 1800 field engineers whom Schlumberger employed in North America.

"I feel that my biggest challenge here in the next couple of years is engineering," Strecker replied, referring to engineering research. "So I'm spending most of my time there now." He said that the next day he would join all the engineering department heads for a three-day retreat in California, at which they would evaluate priorities and challenges. Riboud suggested that the engineers might want to consider pushing the manufacturing section of Schlumberger Well Services, in Houston, which produces 60 percent of the equipment used by the Schlumberger field engineers. Even though this is more than the company's other manufacturing plant, in Clamart, France, produces, Riboud is not satisfied. He wants Schlumberger to become totally self-sufficient—to farm out less work to such companies as Grumman and International Harvester, which makes the frames for Schlumberger's trucks.

There was a long pause. Riboud sat inspecting the fingers of one hand, and finally Strecker asked if Riboud had any further questions.

"I've got a major concern about what happens to your business in the next few years," Riboud said. He then recalled that Strecker's monthly report for January, which he had received in New York, revealed that North American logging operations were 11 percent below plan and that operations in completed wells—so-called cased-hole operations—were 15 percent below plan. "The January report blames the weather," he said. "But then I read and see that the biggest decline was in log interpretation, and you can't blame the weather for that." Although Riboud brought neither notes nor staff assistants to this meeting, he nevertheless was in command of basic facts about Strecker's operations because of two internal reports he receives monthly. On the fifth day of each month, Riboud receives a summary of revenue and net income for each of the major units of the company; on the tenth day of the month, he receives final monthly revenue and net income numbers, with explanatory comments, from all divisions. These numbers are stored in Riboud's mental file cabinets, and quickly retrieved. But Riboud is not an executive who becomes encumbered by numbers and preoccupied with short-term results; he tries to fit the pieces of data into a larger framework, which is what he did now with Strecker. Riboud said he was confident that the world would remain dependent on oil for at least fifty years longer, but he added that two unknowns threatened oil exploration—and thus Schlumberger revenues—in the immediate future. One was the faltering American economy. The other was a decline in the price of oil.

Even in a recession, Strecker said, independent oil

drillers can earn enough to continue searching for oil as long as the price is at least $30 a barrel. He observed that after President Carter began to decontrol the price of oil, in 1979, the number of oil rigs in North America climbed from 2500 to 4750 between 1979 and 1981. "Decontrol caused that rapid growth," Strecker said. But now, with the real price of oil declining, with the economy in recession, and with abundant, if perhaps temporary, oil surpluses, the number of rigs was back down to just under 2500. Strecker said the natural-gas picture was totally different, with supplies plentiful but the price "probably too high."

"It's funny—the gas manufacturers are lobbying in Washington today against decontrol of all gas prices," Riboud said.

If gas should be fully decontrolled, Strecker said, gas producers would not be able to sell all their supplies in this sluggish economy, and the price should drop. (It has not yet done so.) With lower prices, gas producers would concentrate on shallow-well drilling, which was less expensive. Deep-well drilling would become prohibitively expensive, just as it was for independent oil prospectors whenever the price dipped below about $30 a barrel.

Riboud and Strecker, their session over, walked to the office of Robert Peebler, the North American Wireline's vice-president of operations, to review the division's business projections for February. Surveying the expected rig counts of Schlumberger and of its competitors, Riboud seized on the figure of nineteen rigs credited to competitors off the Gulf Coast. "I'm always surprised by how many offshore rigs our competitors have," he said. Peebler replied that competitors had only 10 percent of the offshore market, but this did not seem to appease Riboud; he asked Peebler to forward an analysis of the situation to his New York office. Riboud's message was clear: Only total victory counts. Schlumberger could lose its edge; competitors with more to prove could be hungrier and more aggressive. Already, Wall Street analysts who examined oilfield-service companies had reported that Dresser Industries' Atlas Oilfield Services Group, a worldwide competitor, was leading in the development of the Carbon-Oxygen log and the Spectralog—two advanced logging tools. Gearhart Industries, which was bidding for a larger share of the American market, claimed to have hired 300 graduate engineers in 1981—an increase of 100 percent over 1980. (Because of the drop-off in drilling and the recession, the number fell to 140 in 1982.) Schlumberger remains technologically far ahead of its competitors, but to stay there, Riboud feels, it must continue to challenge its employees.

After Riboud's meeting with Peebler came a slide presentation by engineers and scientists, who talked about such things as a "neutron porosity tool," a "gamma spectroscopy tool," the "radial geometric factor," and the "finite element code." The advanced technology that such arcane terminology represents is perhaps the major reason that Schlumberger stays ahead of its competitors—who concede that Schlumberger's tools are generally more advanced than theirs. And since Schlumberger spends more than $100 million annually on wireline research—a sum greater than the profits of any wireline competitor—its lead will be difficult to overcome.

A portion of the research is devoted to perfecting drilling and logging tools that help identify hard-to-reach oil in already drilled wells and help extract it. This residual oil is expensive to recover, and oil companies claim that as long as the price per barrel stays below $30, pursuing it is not profitable. (This permits them to argue that it is in the consumer's interest to pay higher prices for oil.) But if the price rises above $30, and if supplies become scarce (they are now abundant), new opportunities await the oil companies and Schlumberger. An analysis made by Philip K. Meyer, a vice-president of the Wall Street firm of F. Eberstadt & Company, in April of 1981 explains why: "We have found in the U.S. roughly 450 billion barrels of original-oil-in-place of which only some 100 billion barrels have been produced to date. This means we know the location of 350 billion barrels of remaining (residual)-oil-in-place . . . If only a third of this residual-oil-in-place were to economically respond to tertiary recovery, over 100 billion barrels would be added to U.S. reserves."

Riboud listened intently to the engineers and scientists, and when the presentation was over he said, politely, "I have read all this. You are just preaching motherhood. Where are the problems?"

One problem, Ian Strecker responded, is that there is some duplication between Houston's research operation and the research pursued at the Schlumberger laboratories in Ridgefield, Connecticut, and in Clamart, France. This problem is not new to Riboud. Early in 1982, Jerome Wiesner and Jean Babaud, a vice-president, jointly wrote a "Report on Research and Engineering," covering ten years, for Schlumberger's executive committee, of which Riboud was chairman. The authors praised Schlumberger's research but said that the company's success had brought about "an embarrassment of riches." As a step that would improve coordination, they urged the creation of a new position—vice-president and chief scientist. The man who held it would supervise all research and report directly to Riboud. Wary of bureaucracy, Riboud at first resisted the recommendation, but he later partially changed his mind and, as part of a corporate reorganization, appointed Babaud to a staff job as senior scientist, with responsibility to analyze but not to direct all research.

Not long after the engineering presentation, Riboud had lunch in the executive dining room with three dozen section heads, most of them in their late twenties or early thirties. A number of them said that at Schlumberger they didn't feel isolated in their offices or laboratories, as they had at other places they had worked, and that they weren't dependent on memorandums or rumors to gauge the reactions of their superiors.

"I was at Bell Labs for four years, and I don't think I ever met the vice-president of research," said Dennis O'Neill, who was head of the informatics section and had been with Schlumberger for five years. "Here within six months I was making presentations to the executive vice-president of the Wireline." James Hall, who had been employed by Schlumberger for ten years, said he had had the same experience. "It's a lot more personal at Schlumberger," he said. With a PhD in nuclear physics from Iowa State University and two years of advanced doctoral work at the Swiss Federal Institute of Technology, in Zurich, Hall was the head of the engineering-physics section. While he was completing his studies, he worked for Mobil Oil. "You felt more isolated there, because contact with management was much less," he said of that experience. "You had contact just with your bosses. You didn't feel the direct contact with your managers you have here. It tends to build more of a team spirit when not only your boss comes to talk to you about a project but several levels of command above as well. To me, in engineering that's what the Schlumberger spirit is. The individual design engineer feels that the responsibility of the company is placed on him."

In Riboud's field visits, time is often set aside for questions from employees like Hall. During the lunch in Houston, the first question was from a young engineer-researcher, who asked for Riboud's "view of the non-wireline" part of Schlumberger's empire.

"You are an engineer," Riboud said. "Be a little more precise in your question." Riboud did not wait for the young man to rephrase the question. He apparently sensed that, like many Wireline employees, the young man was concerned about Schlumberger's 1979 purchase, for $425 million, of the Fairchild Camera & Instrument Corporation—which lost more than $30 million the second year after the purchase. Now Riboud went on, "The question is really: When we have this little jewel of a wireline business, why do we bother à la Fairchild and so forth? It's really a philosophical problem. Why does the company have to grow, and in which direction? I'm not saying I'm right, but I feel two things—two dangers. One danger is of becoming a conglomerate and trying to do everything. The other danger is of just staying a wireline company. I don't think we could have maintained the profit margin we had and the motivation of our people if we'd done that. The real problem in any organization is to have new challenges, new motivations."

Riboud then told his audience that employees had also been nervous when Schlumberger branched out into the drilling business, in 1952. Today, the company's Forex Neptune subsidiary is the world's largest oil-drilling company. And employees were nervous again, he said, when, in 1970, Schlumberger acquired the Compagnie des Compteurs, the electric-meter manufacturer. Schlumberger paid $79 million for that company. In 1981, its pre-tax earnings were $67 million. Riboud said that while the Wireline was Schlumberger's chief benefactor, generating 70 percent of the corporate profits, the division could not continue to expand at an annual rate of between 30 and 40 percent, because of the predicted slowdown of the oil business over the next several years. New outlets for corporate energy must be found, he said. In this sense, Riboud subscribes to the views propounded by Thomas J. Peters and Robert H. Waterman, Jr., in their book *In Search of Excellence: Lessons from America's Best-Run Companies*— a book that, incidentally, identifies Schlumberger as one of the best-run companies in the world. "The major reason big companies stop innovating is their dependence on big factories, smooth production flow, integrated operations, big-bet technology planning, and rigid strategic direction setting," Peters and Waterman write. "They forget how to learn and they quit tolerating mistakes. The company forgets what made it successful in the first place, which was usually a culture that encouraged action, experiments, repeated tries." Thus, Riboud said, Schlumberger acquired Fairchild in order to prepare for the high-technology revolution transforming industry and the workplace. Similarly, seeking new corporate energy, Schlumberger had expanded its operations in the Far East, with separate management, research, and manufacturing branches. Now wireline operations in the Middle East reported to an office in Japan instead of to the Paris office. "We keep saying Schlumberger is a multinational company," Riboud continued. "That's not true. We are a combination of Frenchmen and Americans. Not a bad combination. But, fundamentally, in the 1980s we cannot ignore the rest of the world and the Pacific Ocean." Riboud believes in what Mike Mansfield, the American ambassador to Japan, has called "the century of the Pacific"—a century increasingly dominated by the products of Japan, Taiwan, South Korea, Hong Kong, and Singapore. Schlumberger must not succumb to a mania for acquisitions and mergers, Riboud said, but it must continue its decentralized operation. It will remain in the measurement-and-information business, he said, and Fairchild's semiconductor technology will be like the keystone of an arch, holding the entire structure together. Riboud said he believed that microprocessors were creating a revolution comparable to the Industrial Revolution, because they provided plentiful and inexpensive intellectual power.

The Fairchild subject had not been put to rest, for another employee then asked about Schlumberger's stock, which had fallen from an all-time high of $87 a share in November of 1980 to $47 in February of 1982.

(It dropped to $34 in August of 1982, and then rose to $49 in May of 1983.)

Riboud replied that he had long ago given up trying to fathom the behavior of the stock market. "I couldn't care less, and let me explain that," he said. "Fundamentally, we must keep in mind that we are responsible on a longer-term basis for the performance of Schlumberger. I say longer-term because one of the things wrong with American industry is its preoccupation with quarterly statements. So the fundamental question is: Where will Schlumberger's earnings be five years from now? If we do our job—that's what I'm concerned about." (In the fall of 1982, however, when the value of Schlumberger stock was $37.75 a share, and Riboud alone had lost about $36 million, he said, "What has happened to the stock market is a real problem. It's never pleasant to see your wealth cut in half.")

Lunch was followed by a session with department heads from the manufacturing division, which employed 950 people and produced $400 million worth of field equipment annually. The heads of the materials-management and purchasing sections presented Riboud with flow charts and graphs showing a steady rise in their productivity, and spoke in the self-assured lingo of American business schools. Riboud's eyes narrowed. He listened politely but impatiently; finally he leaned forward with his elbows on the conference table and explained why the company could not measure productivity by price or sales alone. "Since we are selling equipment to ourselves, it is hard to measure," he said. There was no competition over price or product or speed of production, he said, and their charts were therefore relatively worthless.

Later that afternoon, Riboud met with the twenty-seven executives and department heads who supervise the North American Wireline division. Many of them also inquired about the acquisition of Fairchild and about Schlumberger's stock. And they asked why Schlumberger had organized a division in the Far East much like the one in Houston. Japan and the rest of the Far East, Riboud repeated, are the frontier of the eighties, as Houston was in the late forties and fifties. There are vast reserves of oil in China. The Japanese have moved ahead of the West in consumer electronics and office automation; they are threatening to move ahead in the development of computers, semiconductors, and genetic engineering. Singapore, Hong Kong, South Korea, Taiwan, and Japan manufacture goods more cheaply and more efficiently than the West does. If Schlumberger does not feel the threat of competition in North America or the Middle East, then it will feel it from the Far East. Schlumberger has been so successful for so long, he said, that it risks losing its "intellectual humility." He added, "We have the King Kong attitude."

When he visited Japan in October 1979, Riboud continued, he came away convinced that the giant companies there had discovered how to motivate people and simultaneously provide them with a sense of security. He saw robotized and automated factories with unthreatened, satisfied workers. He recalled meeting with the president of Kyoto Ceramics, a company whose sales expanded from zero to $600 million in the space of seventeen years. The company was a model of efficiency, he said, and it had not one cent of debt. The key to Kyoto's success was motivation. "Industry is the great successor to religion," the president told Riboud.

Riboud liked that; believed that it matched the spirit that Conrad and Marcel Schlumberger, and now Jean Riboud, thought essential to the company's success. Schlumberger believed in service, in striving for improvement, in something larger than just individual success or short-term profits. Taken with the wisdom of Kyoto's president, Riboud invited him and his top management team to fly to Scottsdale, Arizona, to the Ribouds' vacation home. Riboud promised to bring his top managers. For three days in April 1981, executives of the two companies engaged in a sixties-type encounter session, exchanging ideas about what components go into success, raising each other's consciousness about what builds spirit, what motivates people. Riboud remembers the president of Kyoto saying at one point: "The best is not good enough. You have to shoot for perfection." He liked that, saw it as a motto that would keep Schlumberger humble, force it to measure success not by how well Schlumberger fared against competitors but how well it performed against an ideal. "What you learn is the basic philosophy—what I call the Schlumberger spirit—is very close," said Riboud. Then, with a twinkle in his eye and a slight smile, Riboud added, "Also, I have in the back of my mind that one day we will do something with Kyoto Ceramics."

The next morning, Riboud traveled by helicopter to Schlumberger's new Perforating Center, at Sandy Point, thirty miles south of Houston. The property, 189 acres of open land, is rimmed by concrete bunkers; the smell of gunpowder is in the air; and explosions go off intermittently. Here Schlumberger each year manufactures up to a million and a half shaped charges. (Every two-hundredth charge is detonated as a test.) A typical charge is the size of a pear, and consists of a cone-shaped copper liner dusted with explosive powder which is slipped into a steel shell. When the charge is detonated, a metal jet pierces the casing and the outer wall of a producing well, permitting oil or gas to flow in. Since almost all producing wells have been protected with steel and concrete casings to prevent collapse and to keep out other fluids, the only way to penetrate such a well and tap the oil without destroying its walls is with a shaped charge.

Riboud toured the center and then went to the company cafeteria, where he had coffee with several dozen employees. Gene Pohoriles, the general manager of this unit, was a veteran Schlumberger engineer and, like many old-timers, wore in his lapel a gold Schlumberger pin, with stars that symbolize the number of years he had served the company. Pohoriles introduced Riboud to the employees and then asked the first question: Why did Schlumberger dilute the value of its stock by buying Fairchild?

"Let me be blunt about it," Riboud answered. "What people in the Wireline are asking is: Why did Riboud screw up the Schlumberger stock by purchasing Fairchild?"

"Close," Pohoriles unflinchingly said.

Fairchild was a necessary acquisition, Riboud told him. "I felt strongly that twenty years down the road we had to have a semiconductor capability." He said that because Germany had not invested in semiconductors it had become a captive of Japanese and American computer technology. Schlumberger's basic business, he went on, is information, not oil, and what the Wireline does is provide information to oil companies to help them make accurate decisions. The next generation of wireline and meter equipment, he said, will be more dependent on tiny microprocessors and semiconductors, and he predicted that in five years Fairchild would be "among the top five semiconductor companies in the world, including the Japanese."

5

SHAKING THE TREE

Four days after Riboud had arrived in Texas, he boarded the company jet to return to New York. The trip had served three purposes, he said on the flight. "One, it gives me a certain general feeling for the ambience, the people—how they feel. Two, it gives me a specific judgment on a certain number of people. Three, it permits me to judge certain business problems. I get a lot personally out of this. The question-and-answer sessions are helpful. One way to test people is by the questions they ask—by the freedom or lack of freedom of their questions. The field people are a lot freer than the headquarters people. And the Europeans are a lot less disciplined than the Americans. Americans are careful. Take the session yesterday with the manufacturing people. The stuff I heard— the management-school type of thing I heard—was quite illuminating. Whereas the conversations I had with the engineering people were good." He particularly praised feisty Gene Pohoriles.

Riboud's reactions to Pohoriles—admiring his courage while excusing what Riboud thought was an ignorant question—hinted at Riboud's style of management at Schlumberger. On several occasions, he has said that the company's goal should be "to strive for perfection." To this end, he searches for fighters, for independent-minded people who don't, in his words, "float like a cork." In 1974, when he appointed Carl Buchholz his vice-president of personnel, it was largely because Buchholz was not afraid to speak out. Riboud recalled first seeing Buchholz at a Schlumberger management conference near Geneva. "All the people were reciting the Mass, and suddenly Buchholz said, 'You're full of shit!' I said, 'This is a fellow who speaks his mind.'" The subject under discussion at the conference, Buchholz later recalled, was the development of managers. The executives in attendance rose, one after another, to congratulate themselves on their success, and finally Buchholz stood up and said that in fact the executives were not successfully developing managers at all. A debate ensued and Riboud sided with Buchholz. Afterward, Riboud made a point of getting to know him, and not long after the conference Buchholz, who had been assistant vice-president of operations for Schlumberger Well Services, in Houston, was promoted to vice-president of personnel and transferred from Houston to New York, where he quickly developed a reputation as an in-house gadfly.

In this respect, Buchholz was like Roland Genin, chairman of the executive committee, a gruff former engineer who does not hesitate to disagree with Riboud; or like Aime Vennema, one of Buchholz's predecessors. Vennema held a series of posts, including head of international electronic and measuring services, chief of staff, and chairman of the executive committee. He became what Riboud calls his "American conscience." Vennema and Buchholz are from the Midwest; they are men of simple values, Riboud says, who have "the courage of their convictions." Claude Baks, of Schlumberger's Paris office, has observed, "Vennema was one of the few who dared to tell Riboud what he didn't want to hear." Executives would go to Vennema to test an idea before taking it up with Riboud, and if Vennema didn't like it he would simply make a rude noise. Both Vennema and Buchholz performed the role that Riboud wanted them to perform, but they were considered odd, at best, by some colleagues. Employees recall that Vennema never said good morning, and that if you happened to ride up in the elevator with him and said good morning he would grunt as if he were being assaulted. Buchholz was intimidated only by New York City; for the five years he worked out of Schlumberger's New York office he kept his family in Houston and commuted from a room at a Howard Johnson's motel in Darien, Connecticut.

Of all the people who have surrounded Riboud at Schlumberger over the years, probably none has been closer than Claude Baks, who was hired by Marcel Schlumberger as an engineer in 1946. An enigmatic man with a blunt manner, Baks had no official duties, but he could enter any meeting uninvited and he reported only to Riboud. He was born in 1917, in Latvia. His parents were Jewish, and with the outbreak of the Second World War he joined the Free French Army, fighting in North Africa and Europe. On assignment for the company in Venezuela some years after he was hired, Baks met Krishna and Jean Riboud, who were traveling there. When he returned to Paris on holiday, he looked up the Ribouds, and became close to them and their son, Christophe. Riboud, who was then general manager of Schlumberger's European operations, had a hand in getting Baks transferred from Venezuela to Paris, where he was given a staff job. Admiring Baks' independence, Riboud asked him to become his adviser. At this time, Riboud, with Henri Langlois, was raising money to finance a twelve-hour film, directed by Roberto Rossellini, about the history of the world. (They raised $500,000, including $100,000 from Schlumberger.) Baks shared Riboud's interest in film, and worked closely with both Langlois and Rossellini on Riboud's behalf. Baks had no family of his own, and the Ribouds in effect became his family. "My father would send him to India if my grandmother were sick," said Christophe Riboud. "Baks is always there."

Riboud and Baks were an unlikely pair. Riboud is a man of delicate appearance and subdued manner. Baks has bushy black eyebrows, a stubbly black beard, a bulbous nose, and is missing a few front teeth. A toothpick usually protrudes from his mouth. He has a deep, raspy voice, which some find intimidating, and he is usually wearing a dirty raincoat, and a baggy sports jacket and baggy pants. His office, a cubicle on the fourth floor of Schlumberger's Paris headquarters, was just two doors from Riboud's. He kept the blinds closed and would not open the windows, which discouraged strangers from staying long. The walls were bare, the desk top was clear, and besides the desk the only furniture was two chairs and three metal file cabinets. Yet fellow employees went to Baks' office to try out new ideas, to unearth clues to Riboud's thinking, to learn something of the company's history, to ingratiate themselves with Baks.

"If you compared him to a literary character, he'd be Falstaff," observed Jean-Claude Comert, a former French journalist who manages the communications department in Europe under André Misk.

In trying to explain the role that Baks played, Riboud has said, "His main contribution at Schlumberger has been to prevent Schlumberger from becoming an establishment." He went on, "He has never had a title in thirty-five years. He has never had a secretary. He has never written a letter. He has no responsibilities. Schlumberger is not a bank where everyone has to have a niche. Over the years, he's had more purpose than ninety percent of the people I know. He forces people to think." What Baks helped do was keep alive, under chairman Riboud, a sort of permanent "cultural revolution" at Schlumberger.

In 1982, there was considerable speculation about Baks' future—particularly after Riboud's reimposition of a mandatory retirement age for the board of directors. In July, Baks would turn sixty-five, the mandatory retirement age for employees, and associates wondered whether Riboud would stretch the rules for him. On being asked about this in the spring of 1982, Baks said, "Maybe I won't leave. Maybe he'll return me as an adviser. He once told me we'd both leave together. But I don't ask anything." In September, Riboud went against the speculation within the company and announced the retirement of Baks.

Baks remains bitter about this, but, like others, he knows that Riboud is a master of the unexpected. "Generally, after a while people repeat themselves," observes Michel Vaillaud, who until he was promoted in December of 1982 was one of two Schlumberger executive vice-presidents for operations, his sphere being all oilfield services. "You know what they will ask you. With him, you never feel safe. Never." Vaillaud, who is fifty-one years old, is a lean, regal-looking man. When he met Riboud, in 1973, he was a career civil servant. He had graduated first in his class from École Polytechnique, which Conrad Schlumberger attended, and which is one of the best scientific schools in France. He then received an advanced degree from mining and petroleum schools, and, entering the Civil Service, rose rapidly in the French Ministry of Industry. When Riboud and Vaillaud met, Vaillaud was the Ministry's director for oil and gas. Some weeks later, Vaillaud recalls, Riboud offered him a position at Schlumberger. Although Vaillaud's training and experience were in petroleum, Riboud asked him to move to New York and become vice-president of Schlumberger's electronics division. Vaillaud spoke little English, and he felt unsure of himself in electronics, but he accepted the offer.

Two months after Vaillaud took the job, Riboud called and asked to spend the day with him in New York.

Vaillaud remembers feeling that he gave inadequate answers to persistent questions from Riboud. "I came back and told my wife, 'We should pack—I'm going to be fired.' Then I heard nothing the next day, or the next." At the time, Vaillaud did not understand that his uncertain technical answers to Riboud's questions were secondary. Riboud was taking his measure as a man, not as a technocrat. Computers could spit out data; Riboud was searching for character. Two years later, Vaillaud returned to France as president of the Compagnie des Compteurs. Then, in 1981, when Riboud decided to divide Schlumberger into two basic parts— the Oilfield Services, and Measurement, Control & Components—Vaillaud and most Schlumberger executives expected him to make Vaillaud the head of the electronics division and Roland Genin, who had been an executive vice-president and manager of Drilling and Production Services, the head of the oilfield division. These appointments would have had a certain logic to them, for Vaillaud had mastered electronics and Genin had spent his career in the oilfield division, beginning in 1950, when he joined Schlumberger as a field engineer. Riboud did just the opposite: Vaillaud became the head of the oilfield division, Genin the head of the electronics division. Riboud picked the less experienced man for each job, because, he says, each would bring a "totally different view," a "fresh imagination" to his new task. Riboud had taken a similar unexpected step two years earlier, when he chose Thomas Roberts, a West Point graduate who had become the vice-president of finance, to be the new president of Fairchild. Roberts had asked him why, and Riboud had answered, "I like to shake the tree."

If an eagerness to shake the tree is one of Riboud's most prominent management traits, another one— allied to it—is, obviously, his preoccupation with personnel matters. As his meetings in Houston demonstrated, he is familiar with people at many levels of the organization. Instead of closeting himself with a few top executives, he meets with large groups of employees. The vice-president of personnel at Schlumberger—the job is now held by Arthur W. Alexander—reports to the president, not to an executive vice-president, as is often the case at other companies. "Riboud spends more time on people and people problems, in contrast to business and business problems, than any other chief executive I've ever seen," says Benno Schmidt. "I think the thing he's most concerned with in running this vast business is coming as near as possible to having exactly the right man in the right place all the time. Most people who run a company are much more interested in business, new products, research—all that."

In some ways—like the late Lyndon Johnson and other skilled politicians—Riboud is an inveterate gossip; always asking about people, storing information, searching for clues that will, in his words, get at "the core of somebody and his real thinking." That is the way mentor Marcel Schlumberger, in his own cantankerous way, ran the company, seeking out individuals like Gene Pohoriles who did not "float like a cork."

When it comes to evaluating individuals, Riboud can be quite blunt. Once a year, he meets with each of his top executives to offer an evaluation of their performance. Carl Buchholz remembers one of his evaluations: "He said, 'Let's talk about the Buchholz problem.' He talked about my relations with other people, and how I ought to improve them. He talked about what he wanted done that wasn't being done. He was quite specific."

Riboud's attention to personnel matters is typified by Schlumberger's management-potential summary, or SLP-1A form, which every manager in the company completes once or twice annually. The form, which consists of a single page, asks the manager to identify all the people who report to him, and to select two or three who are "ready now" to take over their supervisors' jobs, and two or three who will be "ready in the future." The manager must give a grade—A, B, C, D, E—on employees' performance, and the form provides spaces for their age, potential, years with the company, months or years in their present job, and the date when they will be ready for promotion. The form must also be completed by the executive to whom the manager reports, so that there can be double evaluations of people before promotions are made.

This form came to my attention when Larry Hinde pulled a copy from his briefcase at Orly Airport in March 1982. At thirty-four, Hinde was the $180,000-a-year vice-president in charge of Wireline Atlantic, which then supervised all oilfield services in Europe, the Middle East, Africa, and South America. Hinde was a Riboud favorite, a Saturday golfing partner in Paris, a self-confident American from Artesia, New Mexico, who wore cowboy boots to work and managed 4800 employees, including a deputy twenty years his senior, with a combination of firmness and finesse. At the mention of Hinde's name, one of the first things Riboud thought to say was how, on his second day at work at Clamart, France, Hinde ordered the executive dining room closed. From that day on Hinde ate in the company cafeteria. As he waited for a plane to take him to a Houston conference, Hinde spoke of the SLP-1A form as if it were the Holy Grail. "It forces managers to evaluate people," he said, explaining that it also helped him to evaluate the judgment of those reporting to him because he could compare his assessment of people with theirs. He could call in each manager to discuss their report, providing another measurement of their judgment. And the form compelled Schlumberger and its executives to think, constantly, about succession. If something happened to him, said Hinde, the company could consult the SLP-1A form.

Sadly, a week later the form was consulted to help locate a successor to Hinde. After attending the conference in Houston and visiting his parents in New

Mexico, Hinde stopped off in New York. His body was found on March 28, 1982, in bed in his room at the Waldorf Astoria, the cause of death at first listed by the Police Department as due to "natural causes." More than one year later, New York City detectives announced that Hinde was killed by a lethal dose of the drug scopolamine, and then robbed. The SLP-1A form on Larry Hinde, filled out by D. Euan Baird, executive vice-president for the Wireline, awarded Hinde the highest rating. (In fact, Riboud saw Hinde as a leading candidate to become president of Schlumberger after Riboud, and his immediate successor, retired.) Hinde's own SLP-1A form chose as his successor Roberto Monti, a forty-two-year-old Argentine. Monti was Baird's choice.

The SLP-1A form springs from a central management principle at Schlumberger: decentralization. This principle accounts for the small number of people at Schlumberger headquarters and for Riboud's clean desk and quiet phone, and his unwillingness to issue orders to Strecker, or to his manufacturing division, or to other executives. Decentralization is not, of course, solely a matter of choice. An oilfield-service business operating in ninety-two countries on five continents must decentralize. An official working out of Schlumberger offices in Paris, New York, Houston, or Tokyo cannot cope with all the clients and questions. "You deal with a client," says John Kurzeja, a twenty-eight-year-old former engineer, who was the manager of a Schlumberger training center for engineers in Belle Chasse, Louisiana. "You fill out the invoices for our services. You're given millions of dollars' worth of technical equipment to operate. You're operating the client's million-dollar oil well. You're it! When you walk out on that rig, you're Schlumberger!"

6

AN ENTREPRENEURIAL COMPANY

Schlumberger services some 85 percent of all the oil rigs operating in the Gulf of Mexico from its Belle Chasse center. At another area of Belle Chasse, fifty workers rebuild vehicles called skids; a skid costs $550,000 and relies on powerful computers to process well-log data in the field or transmit it to data centers. These skids are used on oil rigs in the Gulf, and, like the Schlumberger trucks on land, carry five-ton winch drums with 18,000 to 23,000 feet of wireline cable on them, and backup electrical generators.

The training center at Belle Chasse recruited 137 electrical-engineering graduates in 1981. For all recruits, the routine was the same: up to three weeks of orientation on an oil rig, followed by three months at the training center. Here they were given on-the-job training, using their own well and rig and several units to generate their own logs. If they succeeded, graduates became junior engineers and were sent into the field for six months of intensive on-the-job training, under the supervision of an experienced engineer. Over thirty months, they had to return to a training center for five weeks of advanced instruction, and once a year, before receiving a promotion, they had to take an oral examination, standing before a group of evaluators and giving a formal talk on log interpretation and the use of tools. Then they were subjected to hours of rigorous questioning.

A field engineer's work typically begins when his beeper goes off. He calls a dispatcher to learn his assignment. He goes to the office to collect his tools and a two-member crew, and within hours is on a chartered boat or a helicopter speeding toward an offshore rig. Speed is essential, because the client is paying upward of $200,000 a day to maintain an offshore rig, and has to stop drilling until the Schlumberger engineer answers certain questions or solves a particular problem. The engineer orders his cable and sonde lowered into the well and sits hunched over an eleven-inch rectangular screen, whose readings can tell him, at each depth, where the oil or gas may be, the type and thickness of the rock formations (thicker formations often mean less water and more hydrocarbons), the porosity of the rocks (the more porous, the more oil the rock holds), the permeability of the rock (how well the oil will flow from the rock), and the slope and shape of the oil reservoir (which helps the client figure out where to drill). Other perforating tools provide oil, rock, and sand samples. Each measurement is called a "job," and the Belle Chasse engineers average close to four jobs on each trip to a well. The average trip lasts three and a half days, and the normal Schlumberger bill for this is $50,000.

There is both rigor and danger to this work. Like baseball players reliving a clutch hit, every engineer savors his favorite perilous story. John Kurzeja remembers being tied to an anchor buoy for eighteen hours in twenty-six-foot seas with winds gusting to fifty miles per hour. But, he is quick to add, "You're compensated for your working conditions."

In early 1982, before drilling activity slackened in North America, the typical first-year American engineer earned $32,000 in salary and bonuses; in the second year, he or she averaged $50,000. Money is not the engineer's only reward. "You have to decide if your log is good enough. That's an expensive decision," says Alex Knaster, a senior field engineer who emigrated from the Soviet Union seven years ago. The oil company needs quick but sure decisions. The Schlumberger engineer must decide whether to recommend another measurement log, whether he has interpreted previous logs correctly, whether the hole should be cleaned and the measurement repeated. "Once you're out there, you have no one to fall back on," says Nancy Ern, a senior engineer from Virginia, who is one of about thirty female Schlumberger field engineers worldwide. "It's given me a lot of confidence."

Over bowls of gumbo and plates of fried catfish, their colleague Dan McLearan chimed in, "The thing that drew me here was that no other job gives you the responsibility you are given here right out of school. All of a sudden you have a crew of people you are responsible for, a lot of expensive equipment, and what you do determines the company's success. All these people trust you right out of school to make money. Your self-confidence grows. You get the feeling you can do anything you want to."

These are words which take on more meaning while watching William Blake perform. Blake, twenty-five, parked his Schlumberger truck at 5:30 A.M. in a muddy lot covered with weeds just 200 or so feet from a four-lane highway in Belle Chasse. In Louisiana, if a site is at least 300 feet from the nearest building and does not imperil water pipes, landowners are free to drill for oil. Which is what Louis Lemarie and several partners who own this plot of land are doing with the assistance of a small, rusty rig, equipment that costs about $15,000, and Schlumberger engineer William Blake. Inside the cabin of his Schlumberger truck Blake paid no attention to visitors, including his division manager and Schlumberger vice-president André Misk. He remained hunched over his console, studying the wiggly lines produced by the sonde as it inched its way down the well. Bending over his left shoulder was an anxious Lemarie, intently studying the wiggly lines that look like an electrocardiogram. There is total silence. Minute after minute the line produced remains uniform, indicating that the sonde is passing through rock filled with salt water, which conducts electricity. Suddenly the line swings wildly, kicking sideways, indicating high electrical resistivity, which means the sonde is passing through something that does not conduct electricity—perhaps oil-bearing rocks.

"See that shaley stuff. That's good," Blake tells Lemarie, who is twice his age and a trained geologist. Removing his white hard hat and turning to face Lemarie is a smiling, babyfaced young man with straight blond hair cascading to his shoulders, a thick mustache caked with mud, as are his blue overalls. Blake announces, with the self-assurance of an experienced surgeon, that he is encouraged but wants to take additional measurements to be sure it is oil. Later, acting as salesman, he will try to sell Lemarie additional sophisticated measurements. Blake gives a perfunctory hello to his visitors and returns to his console, telling his operator to raise the sonde to another depth to continue the logging of the well. Pleased, Lemarie lights his pipe and leaves the cabin.

"Watching that screen is nerve-racking," Lemarie says, standing in this weed-filled lot he owns and watching automobiles whiz by. "I used to like to open up a chart and look at the whole thing. Foot by foot is nerve-racking. It looks like we have a nice well here. Which probably gives us room for one more rig up the road." He guesses that "the well we're looking at here ought to make about one hundred barrels a day." The simple Schlumberger log Blake has just taken will cost him $25,000. But at the then $33 a barrel price the well should produce $3,300 daily, $100,000 monthly. The total cost of logging and drilling and maintaining this well will be repaid in three to four months. A small investment, he says, when you consider that the well will gush oil for years.

Why did Lemarie and his partners hire Schlumberger, the most expensive logging firm in the world? "They're basically ahead in research and development," answers partner Dick Boebel. Schlumberger equipment can better withstand well temperatures that reach 400 degrees Fahrenheit and pressures of up to 20,000 pounds per square inch, he says. Jim Londram, another partner, concurs. He tells of once hiring another wireline firm and: "Everything failed. It took us two days to log a 10,000-foot well. Schlumberger has real good backup." Schlumberger monopolizes the wireline business, he adds, because they are the most experienced and the best company in the business. Did these wildcatters find it uncomfortable to rely on the judgment of a babyfaced engineer who, without his Schlumberger overalls and hard hat, might be dismissed as a hippie? Not at all, says Lemarie. Younger engineers "have an enthusiasm level"; they work harder and are more open to new technology and to asking questions; they haven't shed their humility.

Engineer Blake worked through the day and night, finishing the log at 1 A.M., then giving clearance to set pipe and produce oil. At one point he started to perform a more sophisticated logging measurement, using a core-gun sample taker to shoot bullets into the rock formation. But the bullets, which are connected to the main wireline, got stuck and tension built on the line. "I suggested to Lemarie that the decision was his but that we should not do another one," Blake said later. His work finished, Blake returned to his New Orleans apartment. Asked in a subsequent interview what he thought of his job, Blake said that when he graduated from Clarkson College two years ago he had never heard of "Schlum-berger," as he first called it. Now this native of Hudson Falls, New York, was earning $50,000 a year, not including a bonus, traveling all over the world on vacations, and getting job satisfaction that money alone can't buy: "It really feels good that they put so much faith in you. I've been thinking of writing out a résumé if I ever wanted to leave the company, and there is no way I could make the same money. And no way I could put down on a résumé that I was responsible for the company making two to three million last year. It's just phenomenal."

One better appreciates the need for decentralization, and the independent spirit it fosters, at places like Ras Gharib and Ras Shukhier—remote camps in the Egyptian desert. The engineers there are on their own. They have no telephones or daily newspapers at either camp, and no bars and no movie theaters. The only way Schlumberger's Cairo headquarters can reach the camps is by two-way radio. In recent years, Egypt has attained oil self-sufficiency—a fact that has gone largely unnoticed. Indeed, in 1982 it produced 650,000 barrels daily, or twice the country's needs. Most of its oil is in the Gulf of Suez, across from the Sinai. In the spring of 1982, Schlumberger was performing services on forty-two rigs in Egypt. In all, according to William Bufton, then the company's division manager in Egypt and the Sudan, Schlumberger claimed 97 percent of all oilfield-service work in Egypt. This work is lucrative for everyone. Bufton says that each offshore rig in the Egyptian fields costs an oil company about $100,000 a day to operate; each rig produces an average of $50,000 a month in field profits to Schlumberger.

"This is what is called a bachelors' location," says Étienne Danois-Maricq, a twenty-seven-year-old Belgian, who supervises twelve engineers and forty-six other employees at the Ras Gharib camp, a five-and-a-half-hour drive from Cairo across a pebbly desert. Engineers work seven days a week for two months, and are on call twenty-four hours a day. Although they are on the Gulf of Suez, swimming is forbidden, both because the beaches contain Egyptian mines left from the 1973 war with Israel and because heavy crude oil from the off-shore rigs has spilled a half-inch film stretching along the beach as far as the eye can see. Like firemen, the engineers wait for the alarm to ring, summoning them to a job. Over the two months, an engineer will make, on average, six trips to a well, each trip lasting two or three days. When the engineers are not out on a job, they hang around the office, check their tools, and fill out invoices. Recreation usually consists of going to the living room of one or another of a row of dormitory-like clay-brick villas they share, at Ras Gharib, or to a trailer remodeled into a recreation room, at Ras Shu-khier, and playing Ping-Pong or cards, planning vacations, or rewatching videotape cassettes of such movies as *Saturday Night Fever* and *Butch Cassidy and the Sundance Kid*, or a tape of rock singer Meatloaf performing a duet with the singer Cher, who slinks and shakes about in tight shorts.

The engineers at Ras Shukhier compare their life to military service—isolated, rigorous, disciplined, intense, boring. Yet they also speak of the rewards. A second-year engineer here, according to Schlumberger officials, receives a base salary of $45,000, not including an annual bonus that averages from $15,000 to $25,000. Engineers in such remote locations receive free room and board and an automobile, and after each two-month stint the company pays the equivalent cost of a round-trip ticket to Rome for a two-week respite. In addition, they have two months' paid vacation annually, with Schlumberger subsidizing the equivalent cost of a round-trip ticket home. But the financial rewards pale, the engineers say, in comparison to the psychic reward of being "your own boss." David Johnson, a twenty-seven-year-old English engineer, says, "You get lots of responsibility at an early age. It's not like a company in Britain, where you're just waiting for someone at the top to pop off. If you are competent and energetic, you'll do well. It's a good feeling to do a job you really feel is important. It can be hard work, but it's really fun."

"It's not a routine job," says an Iraqi engineer named Alaa Mahdi, who is thirty-one years old. "I don't spend the whole day in the office. I don't have two days that are the same. I have much more responsibility than I would in other jobs. The technical side is quite interesting. The engineer has his own unit, his own tools, his own team."

This sort of work attracts and shapes self-sufficient people. Claus Kampmann, a thirty-two-year-old Dane, whose favorite engineering job for Schlumberger was running a one-man operation in Kurdistan, in northern Iran, says of that job, "It was an ideal setup. I was all by myself. I didn't see anyone from Schlumberger for five and a half months. Only one of my operators spoke English. I joined because I wanted to go overseas and have my own show." Today, Kampmann is one of eleven worldwide unit managers, overseeing all Schlumberger wireline activities in the Middle East. His job pays $110,000 a year and comes with a rent-free house, a car, paid vacations, including round-trip fares, and stock options. The company also puts 15 percent of Kampmann's gross salary into a profit-sharing plan. Kampmann does not feel that he works for an impersonal giant company. "Originally, I wanted to travel overseas and get experience and then start something on my own," he says. "But now I think my job is more interesting than if I were on my own and in sales. I have a much broader spectrum, and I have the impression that I'm running my own company."

7

TAKING THE LONG VIEW

Like his predecessors, Riboud wants people at Schlumberger to have a feeling of independence. Day-to-day decisions are left to those in the field. Riboud's job, as he sees it, is primarily to think five, ten, twenty years ahead, and to set the basic direction of the company. This is why he claims to be unconcerned by what he thinks is the momentary slump in Schlumberger's stock. It explains his behavior at a February 17, 1982, meeting of Schlumberger's finance committee. Edward D. Kline, a partner in Forstmann-Leff Associates, sat near the head of the huge felt-topped table in the conference room at the New York headquarters and explained to the committee how his company managed $40 million of Schlumberger's $300 million in employee pension funds. Of the several firms that manage these funds for Schlumberger, in 1981 Forstmann-Leff had the highest rate of return on their investment decisions. A short, swarthy man, Kline spoke rapidly, rattling off statistics in machine-gun fashion. The key, he said, is to "keep flexibility," to keep shifting investments between stocks and Treasury notes and money funds. Kline confidently predicted that oil stocks would climb (they have since generally gone down), and observed, "Basically, you're in a depression on the corporate side," so the way to invest is to play hunches, to keep switching investments so that you have "about a one-hundred-percent" turnover every year in your investment portfolio. Kline is a legal gambler, and proud of it.

Kline's performance, and that of his company, impressed some members of the finance committee, including board member Felix Rohatyn, who shares Kline's gloom about the American and world economy. "I think this guy makes a very good impression," Rohatyn said after Kline was excused. Rohatyn noted that he doesn't just bet one or two stocks but keeps spreading his bets around.

"The fellow is very pleasant, very nice," counters Riboud, "but when I read his selection of securities I find it hard to find a thread."

"They are very nimble, very pragmatic," says board member Paul Lepercq, agreeing with Rohatyn.

"This is exactly 180 degrees opposite of my philosophy," answers Riboud. "To me the only way to play the stock market is to buy two stocks because you believe in a company and its management, and stick with it."

Rohatyn disagrees, asserting that an investment firm like Forstmann-Leff has to play hunches and know "when to sell."

Riboud rises, and before concluding the meeting offers this final word: "In the argument over the *what* and the *when*, I believe the *what* will invariably win over the *when*."

Riboud has, at times in the past, been wrong about the *what*. His introduction to Schlumberger's 1976 annual report, for example, warned stockholders that the jump in oil prices of the prior two years would slow, bringing a decline in company profits. The next year Schlumberger profits soared 34 percent over the previous year. Similarly, in his March 1980 address to the New York Society of Security Analysts, he predicted: "Logging operations will grow faster in the eighties than in the seventies." Today, Riboud predicts: "Schlumberger's oil service profits will probably rise, but not nearly as fast as in the past." Failing to anticipate the recession that has gripped the semiconductor industry for almost two years, Riboud today acknowledges that he paid too much for a slipping Fairchild in 1979—$425 million—and could have gotten a better price had he waited.

However, based on the success of Schlumberger during his eighteen-year-plus reign, Riboud's overall record in judging the *what* is solid. Influenced by the patience acquired at Buchenwald and under Marcel Schlumberger's wing, Riboud's instinct is usually to take the long view. On September 30, 1977, at a celebration of the fiftieth anniversary of the Schlumbergers' first log, he remarked, "I should say that the most important thing I learned from Marcel Schlumberger was to have an independent mind—to think for oneself, to analyze by oneself, not to follow fashions, not to think like everyone else, not to seek honor or decorations, not to become part of the establishment." On another occasion, he told me, "When you fly through turbulence, you fasten your seat belt. The only seat belt I know in business turbulence is to determine for oneself a few convictions, a few guidelines, and stick by them."

Riboud the businessman puzzles many of his nonbusiness friends. For years, Henri Cartier-Bresson has wondered why Riboud worked in a corporation instead of plunging full time into art or politics. Cartier-Bresson—a shy man with pale blue eyes, gold-framed eyeglasses, and close-cropped white hair—recalls asking Riboud, "What are you doing there? You're not a scientist. You have no passion for making money," and that he replied, "I'm a corkscrew."

"It means he knows how a bottle must be opened—

delicately and firmly," Cartier-Bresson says. The cork-screw analogy rings true to many Riboud associates. He is not volatile, like the Beaujolais bottled near his home. Neither Krishna Riboud nor his secretaries and associates can recall one instance where Riboud raised his voice. "He's a very reserved person so it's hard to know when he's happy or not," says his Paris secretary of thirteen years, Jeannine Bourhis. "There's not much difference in his face. He told me once, 'How can you complain about me? I'm always in the same mood.' " When he's angry it is usually camouflaged, betrayed only by the narrowing of his penetrating brown eyes and a stony silence.

When Riboud offers advice, he usually does it quickly and without fuss—delicately and firmly. In Paris recently, Cartier-Bresson talked of Riboud's role in the formation of Magnum Photos. After the Second World War, Cartier-Bresson, Robert Capa, David "Chim" Seymour, and George Rodger decided to form Magnum. Cartier-Bresson was high-strung and brittle; Capa was an impulsive adventurer who would take off on a moment's notice to cover a war on some distant continent; Chim was suspicious and private. Assignments often kept them apart, and there were separate offices in Paris and New York. Inevitably, tempers flared. "We always went to Jean for advice," Cartier-Bresson recalls. "He's a businessman. I remember we went to him once and told him of difficulties between the New York office and the Paris office." Riboud listened without uttering a word while the three photographers poured out their confusion, their frustrations, their bafflement at starting a business. When they had finished, Cartier-Bresson recalls, Riboud said simply, "Nature has not much imagination. Your little problem is the same as Schlumberger's. If you three stick together, it will be all right." His advice turned out to be prescient.

The partners were comforted by this wisdom, and by Schlumberger's contracts with Magnum to provide photographs for their annual reports. Some years later, in 1980, Thomas Roberts had a similar encounter. Riboud, in what seemed like a split second, asked the young finance officer to assume the presidency of Fairchild. "There were no great meetings to say, 'Tom, you have to do this or that,'" recalls Roberts, a man set apart from many Schlumberger oilfield executives because of his smooth manner, carefully coiffed hair, and omnipresent pipe. "He asked, and I accepted. The next time I saw him was months later in San Francisco when I was installed. He spent a few days there and at the end we spent fifteen minutes together and all he said to me was, 'Your job is simple: Fairchild can be number one. You have to find the right people. It comes down to a question of spending more and reducing expenses. And the other tough part of your job is convincing people you have to do both at the same time.' It sounds simple but it crystallizes my whole problem, my whole job."

If he had to sum up Riboud quickly, observes Cornell Capa, head of the International Center of Photography in New York, and brother of the late Robert Capa, it would have "something to do with one sentence . . . Not much bullshit! Maybe that's it."

Even in social situations with friends, the essential Riboud is laconic, his true feelings often hidden. When he comes for dinner to her Paris home he kisses Primrose Gombault on both cheeks, charms everyone with his solicitous questions, his attentiveness, his mixture of self-assurance and softness, his delicacy. But only after he has left, says this fashion designer and wife of the former editor of the newspaper *France-Soir*, does she realize, "He doesn't speak."

"He doesn't like to talk about himself," says Adelaide de Ménil, daughter of Jean and Dominique, and a friend whose Central Park South apartment often provides Riboud with a home-cooked meal when he is in New York. She and her companion, Edmund "Ted" Carpenter, an archeologist, will invite an interesting friend or two, or dine alone with Riboud. "If you ask him a question he'll sort of push it aside," she says. "Once Ted said, 'You should be in politics.' He just said one or two words, and went on to something else." Riboud has spoken not a word of his experiences at Buchenwald to his wife, to his son, or to such close friends as Cartier-Bresson or Claude Baks. Always there is this wall, a wall Lillian Hellman once tried to breach. They had dined together several years ago at a Manhattan restaurant and were walking alone, content after a fine meal with good wine. Hellman felt the moment was ripe and remembers saying, "You've never talked to me about Buchenwald."

"No," responded Riboud, abruptly but softly, "and I'm not going to."

Although Riboud has many friends and is considered to be generous, he keeps a certain distance. Some friends think this is commonplace among successful men who shutter their feelings from friends, and perhaps from themselves. Elizabeth Rohatyn, a close friend who helped get Riboud to her husband Felix's doctor when his lung collapsed in 1981, observes, "The question I always ask Felix is, 'Are you really satisfied with the work you've done?' The Peggy Lee question—'Is that all there is to that?' I always wonder with men like Jean and Felix, what do they feel about themselves, really? What are their real feelings? Both are excellent at giving you cerebral feelings. But I don't know that I have an answer to the question 'How do you really feel about your role as a father? About your wife? About life? About your career?' I only learned a week ago that a male friend of ours has a grown daughter. I knew he had a son; never a daughter. There isn't a woman I know that wouldn't have known that! I can't even get Felix to tell me where he wants to be buried."

One reason Riboud is so laconic, says Jean-Jacques Servan-Schreiber, is that he is a poor communicator.

"He cannot speak. He cannot write. He is a man of profound intelligence who cannot express himself. His dominating quality is that he has a profound instinct for people and judgment. His judgment is important; the way he expresses it is not clear."

To many who know Servan-Schreiber, that is a typical excess. Unlike Riboud, he parades his person and passions—visitors to his comfortable Paris flat are seated in a den before a table laden only with carefully arranged editions of his most recent book (in French, English, Russian, Chinese, Hebrew, Swedish, German, and Spanish). It is true, however, that Riboud is not garrulous, and is rarely eloquent. To friends he gives his loyalty, his wisdom—his ear; he seldom gives his inner doubts, his turmoil—his heart.

Riboud remains a mystery even to his friends. "He is a man who cannot be classified in any way," says Charles Gombault, the former editor of *France-Soir*, who came to know Riboud through Pierre Mendès-France. "Is he an intellectual? I don't think so. Is he a merchant? I don't think so. Is he an industrialist? It doesn't show. He is one of the few men with a strong influence over the president of France, but he will never talk about it. He never shows off. If you see La Carelle, you will understand. It's a beautiful old house with lots of antiques everywhere, extremely comfortable. But if you want to have the feeling of fortune, you do not have it looking at the house. You have it looking at the ground as far as you can see. He is a man of the earth."

8

ROOTS

For a hundred and thirty years, the Riboud family has owned a 1300-acre estate, La Carelle, which is fifty-five miles north of Lyons, in the Beaujolais region of France. The fields and woodlands and rolling hills of this estate form a checkerboard of orange and yellow leaves, green pastures, and brown earth. The farmland is rimmed by dirt paths that meander into groves of linden, birch, fir, pine, American red oak, wild cherry, and mountain ash. The estate includes eight farms, each with a simple farmhouse of earth-colored brick, built in the Romanesque style that was popular six centuries ago. La Carelle is the country home of Jean Riboud.

The main house is a twenty-six-room stone structure, also Romanesque in style, shaded by giant redwood trees. In the center of the house is an atrium with a green-blue-and-black mosaic floor, from which six white marble columns rise, supporting a balcony. A tinted-glass skylight serves as a canopy for this imposing space. The furniture is all of the period of Louis XIV; on the walls are 18th-century French paintings by Vernet and Rigaud. On the main floor are eight wood-paneled rooms, including a billiard room; a dining room with an immense hand-carved table and 19th-century French paintings; and three libraries containing leather-bound books, a number of sculptures and oil paintings, and five generations of family photographs.

In a stone cellar below are a medieval spit and a baking oven; a space where laundry used to be boiled; a small chapel, where Hélène Riboud, Jean's mother, had a Mass said for Jean and his bride, Krishna, when they got married, in 1949; and a wine cellar with perhaps a thousand bottles of Chiroubles Beaujolais—the local wine—and rows of Bordeaux and champagnes acquired by Riboud's grandparents. There is also a modern touch: a screening room, with movie projector, portable canvas chairs, and a felt blanket covering the stone floor.

At the top of a stone staircase that leads from the main floor to the balcony and the bedrooms are several pieces of contemporary African sculpture. The master bedroom is more modern in style than the downstairs rooms, with loud orange draperies and a bright green bedspread. Krishna Riboud has redecorated this room, and is redecorating the guest rooms on the second floor and her workrooms in the attic. On the door of one workroom is a plaque that reads INNER SANCTUM. A door leading to the smaller workroom bears a sign reading ENTER WITH AWE. These two rooms contain Indian, African, and Japanese artifacts and rugs, and file cabinets filled with photographs and textile samples that Krishna, who is an expert on ancient Chinese silks, uses in her work.

Although La Carelle is not home to Krishna Riboud the way the Ribouds' six-room garden apartment, on the Avenue de Breteuil, in Paris, is, she has put her personal stamp on it. "I have never met a woman like her—she could be living in a dreary hotel room and after two days she would bring it to life," Riboud says of her. Krishna Riboud has made a five-acre meadow beside the main house into a sanctuary for a variety of animals, among them fifteen antelopes; four gray sarus cranes, from India, with brilliant red heads; two small gray-and-black Paradise cranes, with plumes that brush the earth: six smaller demoiselle cranes, from the Sudan, their heads tufted with white; four crowned cranes, from Africa; bar-headed geese, from India; twenty species of ducks from different parts of the world; six magnificent white peacocks, from Asia, which stroll in spacious cages; and fourteen blue peacocks, which glide about at will and are often joined by local gray herons.

Krishna Riboud has also helped transform a farmhouse just a few feet from the main house into a home for the Ribouds' son, Christophe, an economist who runs a successful French market-research firm, his wife, Sophie, and their three children. In the colder months, Riboud closes the main house, and when he can get away from Paris for a weekend he stays with Christophe's family. Krishna usually remains in Paris to work on these weekends.

Although Riboud considers himself a citizen of the world—equally at ease in his native France, in the United States, and in India, which he visits annually—La Carelle is the place he calls home. When their father, Camille, died, each of the children inherited a sixth of the estate. After their mother died, in 1957, Riboud bought his brothers' and sisters' land. Of the six children, only Jean and his sister Françoise, who is now sixty-one and lives in a farmhouse a few hundred yards from the main house, enjoyed the solitude of La Carelle. When Riboud bought the property, an arrangement was made whereby the brothers and sisters deeded this farmhouse to Françoise, and there she runs a school and home for handicapped children.

At La Carelle, Riboud supervises a staff of ten, including a gardener whose family has lived in a nearby stone carriage house for a hundred years. Jean-Marie Ruet—"Père," as the Ribouds called the original gardener—lived on the property for eighty-two years, until he died in 1978 at the age of ninety-four. Ruet's son, Jean, who is now sixty-two, has known only one job: looking after the grounds and the elaborate orchard and garden, with plum, pear, peach, and apple trees, raspberry bushes, and vegetables and herbs. Jean Ruet's son Bernard is being trained to replace his father, and Jean Ruet's wife, Jeannette, cooks for the Ribouds and takes care of the house. The Ruets have an easy, informal relationship with the Ribouds. When Riboud is at La Carelle, the Ruets invite him over for a glass of Beaujolais, *biscuits*, and goat cheese made by a neighbor; they chat about the village and the property.

La Carelle is where Riboud relaxes. He went there in the summer of 1981 to recuperate from a collapsed lung and to think about reshaping Schlumberger's board of directors, and he has many times been host there to François Mitterrand. Often, he will put on a tan parka, tuck his pants into tall rubber boots, and set out, with his brown collie, for the woods, pausing on the way to inspect dams and ponds and freshly planted trees.

One day recently, a visitor accompanying Riboud on such a walk asked him, "What does La Carelle mean to you?"

"To ask that is like asking somebody what it means to be in love," he replied. "If you've never experienced it yourself, an explanation can never make it clear to you."

Riboud recounted the time he dined at a New York restaurant with friends, Thérèse and Joseph Mitchell, and Jean Stafford, widow of his good friend A. J. Liebling. The Mitchells had just returned from his family's North Carolina estate, and over dessert Riboud recalls Mitchell saying, "I feel a different man, I've learned something which I'll never forget. I'm no longer afraid of death. To die now, I've understood, means going back to North Carolina, just going back home."

Several years later, on a blustery January night, Riboud rented a Peugeot at the Lyons airport and drove to La Carelle. He was late and tired and speeding around a sharp curve just two miles from home when—"Like a flash I saw a brilliant white patch on the road, like lightning. At the same time the car flew off the road, went up a tree in the forest on the left side, turned around on the roof, turned 180 degrees, and sat down. And that must have lasted two seconds." Riboud vividly remembers the incident and his sole final thought: "All of a sudden I said to myself, 'Well, that's very good. I'm only about three miles from the cemetery.' "

The day after telling this story, Riboud drove a visitor to the cemetery in the nearby medieval village of Ouroux. A tiny, unpretentious square lot bordered by a stone wall and cobblestone streets, the cemetery squats across from a 12th-century Roman Catholic church, which most of the 400 villagers attend. One of Riboud's good friends in the village is Jean-Marie Berthet, who was the mayor when Riboud returned from the war, and who was known to the conservative opposition as "the Communist." In the postwar years, Berthet and Riboud became allies when they served together on the village council, and Riboud still feels a special kinship with Berthet. He now decided to pay him a visit.

Berthet, a burly, red-cheeked man, opened his door onto a narrow, cobblestoned village street, and greeted Riboud with an enormous hug. Then, taking Riboud by the arm, he led him and a visitor inside to say hello to his family, who were sitting around a table in the kitchen, finishing their Sunday dinner. In the dining room, Berthet uncorked a bottle of wine, and the two men seated themselves at the table. In no time, they were in a deep discussion of politics—specifically, the politics of the village council. Riboud said that he was upset about the recent local elections, in which conservative candidates won a majority of the eleven seats on the council. That election may have brought to mind the election of 1977, when Riboud's sister Françoise, who had always sided with him and the political left, and who had been closer to him than any of the other Riboud children, allegedly joined with Church leaders and other conservative forces in an attempt to oust the incumbent mayor, because of what they saw as his insufficient devotion to Catholic schools. At least that's how Jean remembers it. Antoine Riboud has a different recollection: "My sister was more left than my brother." Françoise won a seat on the village council, with 118 votes, and Jean, who had been on the council since 1945, lost his, with 117. They have spoken little since. Jean feels disappointed with his sister; Krishna Riboud, who had felt particularly close to Françoise, feels betrayed.

What prompted this split between sister and brother? Françoise Riboud told her brother Antoine she would speak with me when I visited La Carelle, but no one answered when I twice called and knocked on her door. According to Antoine Riboud, the break was the final severing of the umbilical cord; an act that crystallized hurts reaching back to a youth that flowered into success for Jean, and frustration for Françoise. While her brother found happiness in marriage and career, Françoise lives alone with her fatherless child, in the shadow of her brother's home. "It's the breaking of a triangle," observes Sophie Riboud, "of Françoise who represents his youth and Krishna who represents his manhood."

Riboud pressed Berthet to explain how a conservative candidate had won the recent mayoral contest. Berthet said that he himself had favored a schoolteacher who was, by village standards, a liberal, but that the villagers had apparently been "scared" of this candidate. In some rural French villages, candidates divide along religious lines: those who are "good Catholics" and obey the wishes of the clergy are deemed "conservatives," and those who are more independent of the Church and of local custom are deemed "liberals." Issues of moment in the outside world, both national and international, tend to be eclipsed by local concerns. Nevertheless, during his seven years as mayor of Ouroux, Berthet had consistently raised national and international issues, and he openly identified himself as "a man of the left"—as a Communist.

Why had the villagers not been afraid to elect him?

"I labeled myself a Communist because I thought the Communist Party was the only leftist party," he said, and he went on to explain that during the late 1940s many idealists had not identified with the Socialist Party in France because it had not been as vigorous as it could have been in opposing Vichy and postwar colonialism. Berthet had thought that the Socialists, like the conservatives, were opposed to any fundamental changes, so he saw no outlet for his political beliefs except Communism.

The young Riboud felt that his political choices were similarly restricted. He emerged from the war with fervent convictions about the dangers of nationalism, about the importance of a united Europe and a world government, and about one's obligation to oppose privilege—whether of a so-called master race or of the French ruling class. He was a prisoner at Buchenwald for twenty months during the war, and he had seen his Nazi guards as products of a contagious xenophobia and racism, while from both the Communists and the Christians in the camp he had learned the value of faith in something beyond oneself or one's country. For Riboud, the Communists he met at Buchenwald had been "like a fountain of hope."

However one might define Riboud's politics, he has always thought of himself as "a man of the left," although not necessarily as a Marxist. Of course, to identify as a Socialist in France is not to proclaim oneself Marxist. Some French Socialists are Marxists: many are not. French voters confront a basic choice between aligning themselves with the conservative forces or with the Socialist party, just as in America the basic choice is between Republicans and Democrats. For Riboud, the choice was easy. He was a "man of the left." He wanted to break the shackles of the establishment that had comfortably ruled France for centuries. For Riboud this represented more of an attitude than an ideology. Observes Françoise Giroud, who first met Riboud in 1953, "To be of the left in France means you are not a rightist. It means you are not someone who thinks everything is going well, and who doesn't want to change things." What is often at stake are not sharp cleavages over legislation or specific ideas, but political symbolism. The favored placards of the left denounce the "establishment" and "colonialism"; they extol "the poor," the "Third World," a "united Europe."

The center is narrower in French politics than in the United States. Over the centuries, class structures calcified in France and Europe. Reflexively, most conservatives opposed worker demands; most Socialists supported them. Inevitably, governments swung like a seesaw. From 1936 to 1941, the French people were led by six different governments. From 1945 to 1958, when de Gaulle finally fashioned a strong executive branch, twenty-five separate governments held power. The French working class, unlike their American counterparts, predictably voted with the left. They were not seduced by "law and order" and "social issues," as were Democrats who voted for Nixon and Reagan, or by a fellow Southerner, as were conservatives voting for Jimmy Carter. In France, the choices were often perceived simply as a choice between those satisfied with French society and those who were not; between those who, like Riboud, wanted to see a mass education system replace France's privileged system, and those who wanted to maintain "the right schools."

Not surprisingly, in 1968, when student protests against the conservatism of French society and the government of President Charles de Gaulle spilled onto the streets of several cities, Riboud sided with the students. He was in New York and Krishna Riboud was visiting India when Claude Baks phoned him to report that

Christophe, who was eighteen, had joined the Paris demonstrations. "People said it was a revolution," Riboud recalled not long ago. "My feeling about French society was that it was so set that you had to push hard just to move a few inches." Son and father both pushed. Jean Riboud's protest involved his friend Henri Langlois, the founder of the Cinémathèque Française—an international film library that by 1968 contained an estimated fifty thousand films. Riboud had known Langlois since the summer of 1958, when Krishna, who had met Langlois at Cannes, introduced them. That summer, Langlois was editing a film on the life of Chagall, and a friend brought him and his longtime companion, Mary Meerson, to lunch at La Carelle. The couple stayed on for a month. Riboud was fascinated by Langlois, a corpulent man who devoured great quantities of food and had a huge enthusiasm for movies. Jean and Krishna became ardent backers of Langlois' library.

Unlike Riboud, Langlois was somewhat disorganized. Riboud tried to help him devise systems for cataloguing films and for establishing financial records and a salary schedule for employees, but these efforts were less than successful. Films were lost; the bookkeeping procedures became a tangled mess. André Malraux, President de Gaulle's minister of culture, became so alarmed by Langlois' slovenly habits that in February of 1968 he dismissed him as director. Langlois had mismanaged the film library and its finances, Malraux claimed, and he observed that, whatever Langlois' skills, basic arithmetic was not among them. Riboud and others saw the dismissal as an attempt by the conservative government to rule the cultural life of France. The directors Jean-Luc Godard, François Truffaut, and Alain Resnais defended Langlois, whom they greatly admired. Thousands of actors, directors, producers, and other sympathizers took to the streets of Paris to protest the dismissal of Langlois. On February 14, a thousand riot policemen were mobilized to contain a mass protest on the Boulevard Haussmann. Meanwhile, Riboud was quietly negotiating with the French government as Langlois' representative, even canceling business trips and staying away from his office, sometimes for days. Riboud was obsessed by the battle. Strategy sessions were held at the Ribouds' apartment. Riboud was the low-key general of Langlois' army of supporters, encouraging the troops to "push and push" while, in his words, "at the same time I was saying to Malraux, 'Well, we're perfectly willing to negotiate.' "

Finally, in April, Malraux agreed to restore Langlois to his former post. Only a small group knew of Riboud's role in this. One who did is Mary Meerson. "Riboud paid for everything," she said not long ago, in an interview in Paris. "He was the private foundation, arranging everything. It is thanks to him that the Cinémathèque exists. He mobilized all the banks and industries to provide finances. This museum is unique in the world. Riboud is a great man, and he never sought any publicity for himself. When Langlois died, it was Jean Riboud who paid off his debts." After Langlois' death, Meerson was invited to stay in the home of Krishna and Jean Riboud. They paid her bills, nurtured her spirits. Even today, when she lives alone, she says the Ribouds always keep in touch.

9

RIBOUD AND MITTERRAND

Riboud first met François Mitterrand in the mid-fifties. In those days, leading figures on the left—Albert Camus, Jean-Paul Sartre, Pierre Mendès-France, Mitterrand, Gaston Defferre—gathered now and then to discuss their opposition to French colonialism in Algeria, to de Gaulle, to the French Communist Party, and to privilege and the French establishment. They got together at the Paris office of the magazine *L'Express*, whose editors were Jean-Jacques Servan-Schreiber and Françoise Giroud. Riboud admired Servan-Schreiber and invested in *L'Express*. Although in 1954 and 1955 Mitterrand had served as interior minister in the government of Mendès-France, whom Riboud revered, he and Riboud knew each other only casually. The man who eventually brought them together as friends and political allies was Georges Dayan, a French Jew who had befriended Mitterrand in college and had served with him in the Resistance, and who until his death, in May of 1980, was Mitterrand's campaign manager and closest friend. In 1971, when the Nixon Administration, under pressure at home and from abroad, decided to abandon the gold standard and float the dollar by linking its value to the value of other currencies, Mitterrand, who was then first secretary of the Socialist Party and was planning the second of three attempts to become president of France, knew that he had to take a position on the issue. However, he was not sure of its implications, and Dayan suggested that Riboud might offer solid economic advice.

In August of that year, Mitterrand went to La Carelle and met with Riboud. At lunch, they discussed the currency issue, and then they took a walk in the woods and discovered that they shared a number of interests. Both loved to walk, to watch birds, to talk about art and history. Both were fond of nature and prized simplicity. Both had sons named Christophe. Both had served in the Resistance and had been captured by the Germans. Both believed that technology could bring a brighter future. Both called themselves Socialists. A lasting bond was forged. "From then on," Irène Dayan, the widow of Georges Dayan, recalled, "Mitterrand would always ask Georges, 'What does Riboud think?' Since my husband died, Mitterrand has needed Riboud's friendship, Riboud's intelligence, Riboud's impartiality more than ever. Riboud is not part of the government, so he can talk freely. Mitterrand trusts his judgment. Whenever they meet, they walk together. If Riboud goes to Mitterrand's house, in the southwest of France, they walk for hours in the woods. The Mitterrands often have a private dinner that includes the family, the Ribouds, and me."

Until recently, Riboud's intimacy with Mitterrand was not widely known. Riboud will speak off the record to a handful of French journalists whom he knows, but he says that he has never returned a telephone call from any French reporter to discuss politics. He attends meetings with government ministers at Mitterrand's request, and he regularly writes memos to the president outlining proposals related to the French or the international economy, but he does not advertise either of these activities. "I believe that since my husband died

Riboud has probably replaced him, more or less," Mme. Dayan says. There are those in the government and those at Schlumberger who believe that Riboud will one day join Mitterrand's government, perhaps as prime minister—especially if Mitterrand's new austerity program, which Riboud has grave reservations about, fails to bolster the franc.

Riboud's activities on behalf of Mitterrand—or, for that matter, those on behalf of Henri Langlois—help illuminate the mixture of principle, practicality, and sentiment which war within him, molding his political philosophy. One principle shaping Riboud's Socialism is a desire to remake French society so that people who are born to wealth will not have lives of unearned ease. "Profit should not be the only element in judging human life," Riboud says. "It should be one element, but not the only element." Riboud says that he wants to democratize French culture—one reason that he supported Langlois and is devoted to modern art's crusade to redefine the way people see the world. He also wants to spread democracy in the world, and to that end he advocates a united Europe, decries domination by the two superpowers, and champions the Third World.

Another aspect of Riboud's Socialism is practical. In February of 1982, the Mitterrand government began to nationalize companies in five basic industries, including two leading investment banks, eighteen commercial banks, and two major electrical manufacturers—an action that would put the central government in control of 29 percent of French industrial production and 23 percent of the French industrial work force. Nationalization, Mitterrand said, would liberate France from the world recession. Although Riboud was uncomfortable with the nationalization, he reluctantly endorsed it. "I'm willing to pay even the price of nationalization to achieve what Mitterrand wants to do," he said recently. "And that is to establish an alternative to French society—to modify French society and advance a few of the things

I really believe in." Nationalization, he believes, is the practical political price that must be paid to appease the left wing of Mitterrand's party, to keep the Communists weak and without ammunition, and to maintain what he calls "the political mythology."

Riboud once said that "as long as the French Communist Party was strong, conservative forces would be in power for over a hundred years." His enthusiasm for Mitterrand stems partly from his conviction that Mitterrand has humbled the French Communist Party, and that his anti-Soviet views have persuaded French voters that the Socialists are not agents of Moscow. Riboud says that Mitterrand has set adrift the "iceberg" of the French Communist Party, which once blocked electoral success for the Socialists. The Communists' total vote fell from 21 percent in 1969 to just 15.4 percent in the last presidential election, and they were given only four of forty-four cabinet posts in Mitterrand's government. (In a consolidated cabinet, they now hold just two cabinet posts.) "It's becoming absurd to be a Communist in the French society of the eighties," Riboud said recently. "So at one point the break will occur—the whole thing will go out to sea. In fact, it's going out to sea now."

Some of Riboud's detractors claim that his support for nationalization is a luxury denied to many businessmen in France. Some French businessmen, says his close associate Jacques de Fouchier, who is the former chairman of the Compagnie Financière de Paris et des Pays-Bas (Paribas) and is a supporter of the conservatives, "maintain that it's very easy for him to be friends of the Socialists, because *his* company is not threatened by nationalization and he has made a lot of money from a multinational corporation." It is true that nationalization poses little threat to Schlumberger, for in 1982 only 4 percent of the company's operating income and 13 percent of its assets were tied up in France.

As for the sentimental side to Riboud's Socialism, it

springs from boyhood yearnings for solidarity, for reducing issues to choices between the forces of change and the forces of reaction, between good and evil. Inevitably, on some issues Riboud surrenders philosophical coherence to passion. Or as Diana Johnstone wrote of the Cinémathèque protest in the July 1978 issue of *Harper's Magazine*:

> Two political paradoxes stand out. One was that the conventional Left took up the cause of a purely private enterprise against a government intervention aimed only, in fact, at assuring normal management of a public-interest enterprise subsidized by tax money. The other was that the budding "New Left," theoretically in favor of "workers' control" and the free flow of information it implies, ardently championed a one-man control that, however charmingly eccentric, was ultimately tyrannical and mystifying.

The dichotomy between rhetoric and reality, it could be said, has a protracted history in French political thought. Descartes, the 17th-century French philosopher, divorced his commitment to the scientific method from his commitment to Roman Catholicism, proclaiming his dualism with these memorable words: "I think, therefore I am." Down through the years French politics—left or right—has developed a well-deserved reputation for hyperbole. Like many people on the French left, Riboud sees himself as having a kind of moral mission, and thus has a propensity for symbolic battles. While conservatives tend to reflexively side with military regimes, Mitterrand and Riboud instinctively side with governments that proclaim their devotion to "the masses." In his memoir, *The Wheat and the Chaff*, Mitterrand extols Salvador Allende Gossens, the late Socialist president of Chile, as "the first person to join Fidel Castro and Che Guevara in the great struggle that . . . foreshadows a new day in Latin America." Notice that Allende, who believed in democracy, is paired with Castro, who does not.

Like everyone, Socialists have their illusions. By separating what they say from what they sometimes do, the Mitterrand government blinds itself to its own inconsistency: supporting the rebels in El Salvador while at the same time becoming the first Western European government to resume arms shipments to the military junta in Argentina; Mitterrand journeys to Zaire and rails against "imperialism," yet France maintains eight military bases in West Africa and hangs on to the semblance of an empire in eighteen French-speaking African nations. The left is "seduced," writes Kissinger in *White House Years*, the first volume of his memoirs, "by the sentimental illusion" that Third World countries can "be insulated from the physical and ideological realities of the contemporary world through the strenuous exercise of good will." Sometimes their utopian rhetoric collides with reality, as it did for the Mitterrand government when, in its first year, it raised the minimum wage by 25 percent, shaved an hour off the work week, granted a fifth week of paid vacation to all workers, and increased government spending—and helped devalue the franc, slow productivity, and spur inflation.

The left has yet to resolve the riddle of how to accelerate government spending without fanning inflation, how to plan an economy without bureaucratizing it. Because reality has sometimes been unkind to their ideology, Mitterrand's government has retreated from its economic expansionism, substituting conservative austerity measures that sister industrial nations have also turned to as they wrestle with multiple ills—recession, unemployment, slowed productivity, soaring interest rates, and inflation. Like Riboud, his friend Jerome Wiesner began his political life with a set of certainties. He identified with the left. He was convinced that all that was lacking to cure problems was government will. He was innocent of contemporary travails—stagflation, insufficient capital formation, bureaucracy. He thought government was only about ends, not means. Today, admits Wiesner, former science adviser to President Kennedy and president of M.I.T., "I'm thoroughly confused. If someone asked me to run the government, I'd run like hell . . . You start with a bunch of ideas and then find that the world is more complicated."

Riboud's associates have commented on his sentimental insistence that he is a Socialist. "It's a dream of any schoolboy to be a rich capitalist and also to be accepted by Socialism," says Executive Vice President D. Euan Baird. "I frankly think it's a little naive." And Jacques de Fouchier says of Riboud's politics, "It's important in his life, because it's a mood. You know, sometimes you say such and such a thing just when you're in a certain mood. When you have said it enough, you begin to believe it." Françoise Giroud believes that he chooses to overlook the fact that he is a member of the establishment he ostensibly opposes. "He is an intelligent man, but I think his political involvement is purely emotional—irrational," she says. Claude Baks, like Euan Baird, thinks that Riboud is politically naive. "He believes he's a Socialist," Baks has said. "He's not. He believes in equality. Let's say he's a left democrat." And Servan-Schreiber speaks of Riboud this way: "He doesn't know what he means. He is a man who is very unhappy with the state of society. He wants to change it, in a vague way. He does not know how, but he calls it Socialism. He would have been part of the New Deal. He really is outraged about the poor. He's not profoundly political. It's more a moral attitude."

Riboud himself reluctantly concedes that "Socialist" is not a word that adequately characterizes his politics. "To be a Socialist in France today is fundamentally to be a liberal democrat opposing the conservative forces," he said when pressed. "To be a Socialist in France is to try to have some concept of the future." Riboud also concedes that Mitterrand's domestic policies are "a gamble," in that they expose France to the risk of the kind of stifling bureaucracy and steep taxes that have afflicted Britain's welfare state. But if the gamble pays off, he says, and the Mitterrand government is able to shift funds for long-term research to nationalized industries, it will be able to move France into the forefront of technology. Over the next five years, the government plans to invest $20 billion in research and development in electronics alone. Riboud believes that Franklin D. Roosevelt saved capitalism from itself, and he believes that Mitterrand can do so in France. He embraces Mitterrand's push to make the tax system more equitable. "For the last twenty years, France has been the only industrial nation with negligible capital-gains and estate taxes," Riboud says. "And I don't think you can run any tax system without some meaningful form of either a capital-gains tax or an estate tax." Although he worries that the left will one day take these taxes too far, his greater fear is that nothing will be done about French taxation. "The conservative forces have never even tried to do anything about it," he says.

Riboud's concern is tempered by a sense of history. The French are traditionally more relaxed about big government than Americans are. As early as the 16th century, Louis XIV sponsored the formation of state-owned industries. After World War II, the conservative de Gaulle government nationalized much of French banking. As an example of a prevalent American attitude, Riboud cites Ronald Reagan, who declared in his inaugural address that "government is the problem." Riboud says that the American view that all nationalized companies are badly run and all private industries are well run is a vast oversimplification. He notes that the Renault automobile company was nationalized years ago, and it remains one of the better-run companies, and that the same can be said of Air France and Électricité de France, both of which are nationalized. On the other hand, the nationalized British Leyland has been a failure. And nationalizing an innovative company like Hewlett-Packard or IBM "would be a disaster and absurd," Riboud says, adding, "If you were to nationalize a utility like Consolidated Edison, I don't think it would be any better, but I'm not sure it would be any worse." It did not pass unnoticed by Riboud that when the government of Mexico nationalized its banks, in the summer of 1982, American bankers cheered loudest, applauding this action as a commitment by the government to meet its debt obligations to the banks.

To many people, whether in France or in the United States, it seems odd to see a successful capitalist like Riboud espousing Socialism. Riboud, however, views himself as a man seeking fresh approaches that blend a conservative's fiscal caution and belief in strong management with a liberal's compassion and commitment to change. In his lengthy memorandums to Mitterrand, Riboud has urged a "third way"—between a completely state-dominated economy and the austerity put forward by such leaders as Ronald Reagan and Margaret Thatcher. In March, when Finance Minister Jacques Delors argued successfully that the Mitterrand government should try to bolster the sagging franc and close the nation's trade deficit through fresh austerity measures, Riboud was one of those leading the internal opposition. While he supported the program, he did not think it was comprehensive enough, and he urged the adoption of temporary protectionist policies to keep foreign goods out, and an incomes policy to guarantee employment and government-backed credit to businesses; in exchange, he proposed wage concessions from labor and price ceilings from business. Riboud advocates a government-planned and government-financed industrial policy, in which government would approve plans and provide loans while businesses would commit themselves to moderating prices and to innovation.

Such a policy—which parallels, in many ways, his friend Felix Rohatyn's suggestion of a new Reconstruction Finance Corporation to help rebuild American industry—invites questions. Would government decisions about particular industries be made by elected officials or by so-called nonpolitical officials? Why would their decisions necessarily be wiser than those dictated by a free market? Where would the capital come from? If government resources were limited, would subsidized industries receive preferential credit treatment over nonsubsidized industries? If a conflict arose between politics and profits—over whether to move a plant to a new location to take advantage of lower labor costs, say—would the business executives be free to make the decision? And if they weren't, would this arrangement not merely be Socialism by another name?

Though Riboud is somewhat vague about how the system he envisions might actually work, he is clear about its broad contours. He believes, for example, that government must serve as a referee between various interests and the public. Unlike many socialists, he also believes that the waste and bureaucracy of the French welfare state should be reduced. While he favors protectionist measures to safeguard French industries, particularly against Japanese imports, he also favors renewed efforts to create a common European monetary system and to improve international cooperation worldwide. (How to square these seemingly contradictory notions remains a mystery.)

Above all, Riboud retains the optimism of his youth, and Schlumberger has strengthened his belief that conviction and vision are rewarded. The underlying theme of his advice to Mitterrand is that although the problems of France and the world are complex, all that is needed is will and a political constituency. "To succeed, one must be bold yet firm," he concluded one memorandum to Mitterrand.

10

THE CAPITALIST AS SOCIALIST

Riboud sees his work at Schlumberger as an extension of his political views. "Running a company is like politics," he says. "You are always balancing interests and personalities and trying to keep people motivated." On being asked how he would like to be characterized as an executive, he replied, "I would like it to be said that I'm bringing about in my professional life what I'm trying to bring about with myself—it's one and the same thing." Like Marcel and Conrad Schlumberger, Riboud thinks of the company as an extension of personal values—humility, loyalty, preserving faith in an idea, serving people, being trusting, being open-minded to different cultures, being ambitious and competitive and yet mindful of tradition. The key in a corporation or in government, Riboud says, is "motivating people" and forging a consensus. "We are no longer in a society where the head of a corporation can just give orders," he says. People need to believe in something larger than themselves. To be successful, he thinks, a corporation must learn from the Japanese that "we have the responsibility that religion used to have." A good company must not be just a slave to profits; it must strive to perform a service and to beat its competitors. But more, he feels, it must measure itself against a higher standard, seeking perfection.

Riboud's fears about Schlumberger becoming an establishment are clearly linked to his political philosophy. As he worried that Roy Shourd had grown too complacent as president of the North American Wireline, so he held Valéry Giscard d'Estaing in contempt partly because of the former French president's love of pomp and ceremony. "Part of his disdain for people's pompousness is connected with Jean's philosophical view," observes Elizabeth Rohatyn. His views on modern art flow naturally from this attitude. "The only problem I have with modern art," he says, "is that it's been too successful too fast. Picasso was not appreciated until he was sixty-five; Max Ernst until he was sixty."

Building on a tradition started by Jean and Dominique de Ménil, who helped induce Philip Johnson to design Schlumberger's research center in Ridgefield, Connecticut, under Riboud Schlumberger has supported artists, from the photographers at Magnum Studios to the modern artists whose work greets visitors to Schlumberger's Park Avenue offices. A giant Robert Rauschenberg collage announces itself over the head of the forty-fourth-floor receptionist. The adjoining reception room is dominated by a stark white Louise Nevelson sculpture. A Matta canvas swallows almost an entire wall of the nearby conference room. The stark statements of assorted modern artists, many on loan from the de Ménil Foundation, decorate the walls of executives. Unlike Renaissance art, which celebrated the certainty of what the artist saw, modern art, beginning with Cézanne, brought another question to bear, a question Riboud is comfortable with. "But with Cézanne," writes Robert Hughes in his book *The Shock of the New*, "as the critic Barbara Rose remarked in another context, the statement 'This is what I see' be-

comes replaced by a question: 'Is this what I see?' You
share his hesitations about the position of a tree or a
branch; or the final shape of Mont Ste-Victoire, and the
trees in front of it. Relativity is all. Doubt becomes part
of the painting's subject." Doubt, a sense of humility,
is a quality Riboud strives to keep alive at Schlumberger.

Riboud sees Schlumberger as an extension of his political philosophy in another way. He is, says Jean-Jacques
Servan-Schreiber, a truly "multinational man"; simultaneously a Frenchman, an Indian, an American. His
Paris apartment blends various cultures. The complete
leather-bound volumes of Tagore and Proust rest side
by side in the library. The glass doors of the ground-
floor living room open to a lush international garden
laden with trees from various continents. The sparsely
furnished rooms were inspired, says Krishna Riboud,
by "the sense of space" they admire in Japanese ar-
chitecture. The blue and white marble in their separate
baths is from Chile. Because Schlumberger operates in
so many countries and shifts people around repeatedly,
says Riboud, "the result is that it probably changes
quite a bit the tradition of nationalistic feeling or the
sense of belonging to a nation." Riboud is proud that
Schlumberger has never been nationalized, that one-
third of its employees are from the Third World.

Riboud says that with the possible exception of the
oil company Royal Dutch/Shell, Schlumberger is "the
only truly multinational company that I know of."
Schlumberger has long since ceased to have a single
national identity. "If I have one purpose today," Riboud
says, "it is to expand the concept of merging together
into one enterprise Europeans, Americans, and citizens
of the Third World; to bring in Asians, Africans, and
Latin Americans so they feel at home with their own
culture, their own religion, and yet feel that Schlumberger is their family."

*   *   *

Like other multinational corporations, Schlumberger sometimes gets embroiled in conflicts with nations when they uphold their own interests against what Schlumberger says are the world's interests. For example, Schlumberger has challenged the right of the Internal Revenue Service to tax revenues from wireline services performed for companies on the outer continental shelf in the Gulf of Mexico. "We don't consider the continental shelf part of the United States," says Allen D. Klein, Schlumberger's vice-president and director of taxes. In 1980, Schlumberger agreed to an out-of-court settlement on tax claims dating to 1967 and 1969, but in that case the company settled the IRS claim for something less than the $30 million the government wanted, Klein says. Today, Schlumberger is contesting all United States tax levies for work performed on the continental shelf since 1969.

Although in 1982 Schlumberger provided a total of $451 million in taxes to the countries in which it operated (an effective rate of 25 percent), Klein concedes that Schlumberger receives tax advantages from its place of incorporation—the Netherlands Antilles. One advantage involves dividend payments. Any company conducting business in the United States pays a corporate tax of up to 46 percent on its American earnings, whether it is incorporated abroad or in this country; companies incorporated in the United States are required to pay an additional withholding tax of 30 percent on dividends paid to foreigners. However, when companies are registered in the Antilles, foreign stockholders—of which Schlumberger has many—are not taxed by the United States on their dividends.

Klein also says that many American companies have lower effective tax rates than Schlumberger, because they may take advantage of tax breaks not available to foreign companies. But a staff member of the Congressional Joint Committee on Taxation asserts that the tax advantages available to companies that are incorporated in the Antilles can be matched or surpassed by only a small fraction of American companies. In fact, the Treasury Department is now threatening to change a tax treaty between the United States and the Antilles, principally for this reason.

Riboud views his preoccupation with personnel matters at Schlumberger as yet another extension of his Socialist principles. He thinks of Schlumberger as a happy family sharing the fruits of success, and sees the corporation as an instrument of altruism. This view is quite different from that propounded by George Gilder in his book *Wealth and Poverty*, or by Michael Novak in *The Spirit of Democratic Capitalism*. Those two writers argue that capitalism is by definition altruistic and moral because it creates wealth and employs people, and because it makes possible the pluralistic values that keep democracy alive.

Riboud assumes that a corporation has a social responsibility. His son, Christophe, who has a PhD in economics from the Massachusetts Institute of Technology and is extraordinarily close to his father, says a service business like Schlumberger is linked to Socialism because "you can't be successful unless you believe in people—that's what Socialism is all about." Jean Riboud believes that Schlumberger, by providing services to the oil-rich nations of the Third World, has furthered the development and redistribution of the world's wealth. Riboud says he was shocked by President Reagan's across-the-board tax cuts, even though they reduced Schlumberger's American tax liability by $30 million in 1982. (Klein puts the figure at $11 million.) Since government should not forgo its role as referee, he says, these tax cuts were "crazy"; Schlumberger, he says, should have been compelled to show that what it saved on taxes would be invested in capital improvements or enhanced productivity, which would, in turn, generate new wealth.

Of course, the marriage of Schlumberger and Riboud's brand of Socialism is not without its strains. It was not altruism that compelled Schlumberger to incorporate in the Antilles, where it is subject to an income-tax rate of just 3 percent. And it was not altruism that got Schlumberger in legal trouble in the early 1960s—before Riboud became its president—for its role in what became known as the East Texas slant-hole scandal. The victim of this scandal was the Nortex Oil & Gas Corporation, which bought several pieces of land in Rusk and Gregg counties on which it had found oil. By drilling deep slant holes, other oil companies were able to secretly siphon oil from Nortex's oilfields. Schlumberger performed logging and perforating services for the companies participating in this scheme.

Since Schlumberger does not own oil properties, there was no question about whether the company had a stake in this fraud. It did not. But it was taken to court by Nortex and charged with knowledge of the fraud and "conspiracy to commit certain unlawful acts which made the fraud possible." In a November 13, 1968, ruling, the Texas Supreme Court declared that the evidence did not support Nortex's charge of conspiracy, but implied that Schlumberger had engaged in less than admirable behavior. By "the exercise of the slightest degree of diligence," the court concluded, Schlumberger could have discovered the conspiracy. Moreover, it said, "Schlumberger took steps calculated to protect its customers who might be subjected to investigation or to prosecution" by omitting from invoices the depth of the wells it had logged, by destroying pertinent records, and by advising its employees "to have poor memories" when they were questioned. Still, Schlumberger was legally, if not ethically, exonerated.

Although Riboud is quick to denounce right-wing dictatorships and militarism, Schlumberger does a brisk business in Argentina and Chile, among other countries, and several of its subsidiaries have contracts with the French and British governments and with other corporations to manufacture equipment for spy satellites, military aircraft, and missiles. Although Riboud supports a strong, independent Israel, and Schlumberger sells that nation some equipment, Riboud admits that because of the company's work in Arab countries he is grateful that Israel is not in the oil business. Schlumberger executives are extremely nervous that publicity about their non-oil commerce with Israel could jeopardize their extensive business in the Arab world.

Moreover, the interests of Schlumberger, whose profits climb as the price of oil climbs, hardly accord with the interests of most consumers, for whom inflation and interest rates may shrink as the price of oil dips. In a talk Riboud gave to Schlumberger executives working for the company's North American Wireline operation in Houston not long ago, he acknowledged the company's stake in higher oil prices. "What is true is that the future of oil exploration and the future of logging are tied in with the price of crude oil," he said. He claims that there is no contradiction between Schlumberger's desire for higher oil prices and his belief in Socialism, since new oil exploration is in the consumer's interest, and since the consumer also has an interest in a "reasonably predictable price."

One suspects, however, that if the price of crude oil unpredictably jumped from $30 a barrel to $50—far above the price needed to encourage exploration—Riboud would not protest. And if he did, stockholders might protest his continuing tenure.

Although Riboud says that for practical reasons he publicly supported the nationalization of French companies by the Mitterrand government, it might be noted that over the years, with a single exception, Schlumberger has rejected all requests by Third World countries for joint ventures and that it has consistently refused to sell its oilfield-service equipment to any nation (with the single exception of Mexico) or, for that matter, to any private interest.

"I think politics is a contradiction in Riboud," says Bernard Alpaerts, who began his career with Schlumberger thirty years ago as an engineer and retired this year as executive vice-president of the company's Measurement & Control operations worldwide. "Politics is far removed from the management of this company. Schlumberger is almost a company without a nation. Riboud knows very well that most of his managers don't have the same political opinions he has. And, honestly, he doesn't mind. Sometimes you don't recognize in his business decisions the political opinions he has."

The investment banker Felix Rohatyn, an intimate of Riboud's and a Schlumberger director, says, "Riboud is complicated. There is this mixture in the man of being the hard-headed manager of a huge company that is as intensely capitalistic as any organization I know, and at the same time being clearly involved with the Socialist government of France."

This is one of several contradictions in Riboud. He is, for example, a loyal family man—devoted to his wife, to his son and daughter-in-law and their three children, yet he has had sometimes stormy relationships with his brothers and sisters. He takes pride in being open-minded and a foe of bigotry, yet Christophe Riboud says that his father is "one of the most determined and prejudiced men I know." He cited his father's instinctual aversion to members of the establishment—to graduates of the École Polytechnique or of Harvard. Sophie Riboud calls her father-in-law, whom she adores, "a sexist." Riboud guards against Schlumberger's becoming an "establishment," and shifts people regularly to avert complacency; yet for the more than eighteen years he has been president the same rules have not applied to him.

Schlumberger, too, has its share of contradictions. Despite its rhetoric about opposing discrimination, the company has done little to lower traditional barriers to women in the oil business. Among its 2200 field engineers at the beginning of 1982, Schlumberger estimates that only thirty-two were women. Few women are found in oil camps. The well-appointed men's room at Schlumberger's Paris headquarters has fine cloth hand towels; the ladies' room has paper towels. Since Schlumberger's Wireline division has a policy of promoting people from within, if there is no change in policy—no fresh determination to hire women—ten or twenty years from today the company will continue to be dominated by men. "Schlumberger is not a company for women," Jeannine Bourhis, Riboud's Paris secretary, says. "Schlumberger is a company of males. Riboud is making all kinds of efforts to have nationalities represented in the company, and all kinds of skin colors to be promoted. Women are transparent at Schlumberger. They just don't see you."

Although Schlumberger is proud of creating a sense that its employees are all one family, the company nevertheless often disrupts personal family life. Outside North America, the company discourages engineers who are married. The wives of Schlumberger employees, because their husbands are transferred so frequently, find it difficult to pursue their own careers. This difficulty is compounded when families are transferred to poor nations, where jobs are scarce, and to Muslim nations, where tradition holds that women stay home.

"Sometimes you really feel lost," says Kate Yemi, a Nigerian woman whose husband, Esan, runs a Schlumberger computer center in Cairo. "The man has a job to do. You have nothing to do. So you have babies to keep you busy. Or you join a club. If you say, 'I want to have a career of my own,' and say you don't want to go where your husband goes, then you're headed for the divorce courts. That means splitting the children. So you have to decide what's more important—family or your career. For me, the family is more important."

There is also within Schlumberger a natural tension between a desire to keep people on their toes by shifting them regularly, and a desire to make employees feel secure, part of a Schlumberger family. There are fifty-five division managers in the Wireline, who report to eleven unit managers, who in turn report to three vice-presidents. Bill Bufton, then thirty-six, was the division manager for Egypt and the Sudan. In his thirteen years with the company, he had made steady progress, never holding the same job for more than eighteen months. But now he sees the corporate pyramid narrowing: "Once you're a division manager at Schlumberger, you don't have a lot of options left as to what to do." Not only are there fewer top-level jobs in a company that is lean at the top, but there is also the youth factor: Schlumberger seeks to promote young executives. There is irony in this. The company's success is partly attributed to the fact that it provides employees with competitive incentives. The other side of this Darwinian coin, however, is that those who grow older and don't climb that next rung up the ladder get pushed off, or are paralyzed by fears that they might be.

Gunter Hiller, who manages the Cairo Maintenance Center, is thirty-eight, two years older than his boss, Bill Bufton, six years older than the unit manager for the Middle East, Claus Kampmann, and four years younger than North American Wireline Vice-President Ian Strecker. And Hiller admits he is worried about where he will go next. Even if he does a good job, he knows he may get pushed aside for a younger executive of equal talent. His problem is not unlike that confronting thirty-two-year-old pro halfbacks. They may have a couple of seasons of capable play left, but there are only forty-nine slots on the roster and the rookie halfback may have ten years of competition in his legs. "In

Schlumberger, you're either too young or too old," observes Ian Strecker. "I'm just passing from being too young to being too old . . . There are only a few key jobs. So you've got all these young dynamic people coming up and nowhere to put them. Maybe you put them in Fairchild and other places. The answer is not obvious."

Being the biggest and the best wireline—or drilling, or meter manufacturer, or oil-well-cementing company—can be a curse. The line between pride and smugness can be a thin one. Because Schlumberger is so big, Larry Hinde said, "We don't have time to spend as much time as we should with people." Smaller but aggressive competitors like Gearhart Industries, he said, had succeeded in luring away some Schlumberger engineers. Riboud frets about the curse of success, telling his Houston department heads, "We are proud of what we do, and we don't think there is much for us to learn. That's a normal human reaction. To accompany our King Kong attitude we need intellectual humility." Self-satisfaction, he warned, could transform Schlumberger into a safe, establishment company.

The much-vaunted Schlumberger spirit, which engineers speak of with the fervor of an Iranian ayatollah, also carries with it a curse. It creates a "swashbuckling spirit," says D. Euan Baird, executive vice-president of the Wireline; a spirit in which the engineers' self-reliance can slip into overconfidence. The willingness to take risks that makes them good engineers also increases their safety risks. In 1981, for example, there were thirty-seven accidental Schlumberger deaths, two-thirds of them needless automobile fatalities. "My problem sometimes is slowing them down," says Baird, who worries that the engineers sometimes become "short-sighted," an inbred, "too-successful Mafia."

Of course, as Baird is quick to add, that's "a nice problem to have." In fact, Schlumberger is a company with an unusual number of "nice" problems.

11

WHY DOES SCHLUMBERGER SUCCEED?

At a time when attention has been riveted on why U.S. companies fail, it is useful to ask the flip side of that question: Why does a company like Schlumberger succeed?

In order to answer this, one should probably first inquire into the degree of success of Schlumberger's various components. Schlumberger, according to Wall Street analysts, has a near-monopoly on the oilfield-wireline business—about 70 percent of the world market. (Its nearest wireline competitor, Dresser Industries' Atlas Oilfield Services Group, has just over 10 percent.) And Schlumberger retains its near-monopoly even though it charges higher prices than its competitors. "We believe we are entitled to a certain return on investment, which we intend to maintain, and we price accordingly," says D. Euan Baird, who is forty-five, Scottish-born, and, like most of the company's top executives, started as a Schlumberger field engineer. A policy first established by Marcel Schlumberger remains in force today: Schlumberger charges its wireline customers twice the amount of its field costs. Because Schlumberger does not sell, or even lease, its equipment, and because its equipment is the most technologically advanced, so that the company provides the best technical service, it remains the most highly regarded company in the oilfield-service industry. Of course, oil companies can afford to pay its prices. Since the cost of logging a well—the wireline process—is only 2 to 5 percent of the oil company's cost, wrote John C. Wellemeyer, managing director of the investment-banking firm of Morgan Stanley, in 1973, "Schlumberger should be able to increase prices as much as required to maintain its margins." Until the current oil shock, that is what it has done.

"To measure a successful company, you need time—a long span of time," Riboud says. By that measure, too, Schlumberger is a success. Figures on the company's profits were first made public for a full year in 1958, and in all but two years of the quarter century since, its profits have climbed. (In those two years, 1961 and 1963, they fell only slightly.) Profits jumped from $12.2 million in 1958 to $1.35 billion in 1982. Profits rose even when the price of oil did not. Between 1956 and 1972, oil drilling in the United States declined 10 percent, but Schlumberger's wireline revenues went up in all but one of those years. Between 1974 and 1978, Schlumberger's earnings per share more than tripled. One might attribute this success to the luck of being in the right business, except that this does not explain why Schlumberger's profits swelled in bad years, or why they increased by 6.5 percent in the recession year of 1982 while the profits of oilfield-service competitors and of seven of the eight biggest American oil companies declined. (Schlumberger's earnings per share went from $4.37 in 1981 to $4.60 in 1982.) Jacques de Fouchier, who calls Schlumberger the single best company in the world, has pointed out, "You must understand that an ordinary shareholder who in 1965 had one share of Schlumberger, valued in the market at thirty-five dollars, has now—without having had to pay any-thing more in cash—fifty-one shares worth about fifty dollars a share."

Although about 45 percent of Schlumberger's reve-nues and an estimated 70 percent of its profits derive from the Wireline division, the company's success is not attributable to this division alone. Overall, Oilfield Services, of which the Wireline is a part, accounts for two-thirds of Schlumberger's more than $6 billion in annual revenues, while the other major division, Meas-urement, Control & Components, accounts for the re-maining third. Most of Schlumberger's companies have demonstrated a steady growth pattern, with recession-ary 1982 being a notable exception. The company ac-quired the Compagnie des Compteurs in 1970 and eventually renamed it Measurement & Control–Europe; it is a subsidiary of the overall Measurement, Control & Components division. At first, its profits rose slowly; then they gained steadily. John H. Hayward, Jr., vice-president of fundamental research at Merrill Lynch Pierce Fenner & Smith, has written, "Operating margins in-creased from less than 2 percent in 1971 to about the 11 to 12 percent area in 1980." Today, Measurement & Control–Europe is the world's number-one manufac-turer of electric meters and ranks first or second in the production of water and gas meters; its national cur-rency revenues rose 18 percent in 1981 and 13 percent in 1982. Another company, Forex Neptune, is the world's most profitable oil-drilling service; its revenues jumped 28 percent in 1981.

Gauged by profits alone, Schlumberger ranks among the premier companies in the world. If it had been eligible to be included in the 1982 Fortune 500 listing of the biggest American industrial firms, it would have ranked thirteenth in profits—above Gulf Oil, Procter & Gamble, Eastman Kodak, and Philip Morris, for in-stance. Among the Fortune Foreign 500, only four com-panies earned larger profits than Schlumberger in 1981.

And none of the world's thousand industrial giants rivaled Schlumberger's 1982 net income as a percentage of revenue of 21 percent of revenues (or sales). In 1981, Exxon, the world's largest industrial corporation, earned profits of less than 5 percent on sales of $108 billion. IBM, which ranked second in the United States, earned profits of 11 percent on sales of $29 billion. The Royal Dutch/Shell Group, the largest overseas conglomerate, earned profits of 4 percent on sales of $82 billion. The median return on stockholders' equity of the 500 largest American corporations was 13.8 percent; Schlumberger's was 34 percent.

What accounts for a company's success? *In Search of Excellence* identifies eight traits shared by the fifteen "excellent" American companies they studied. The companies were: Bechtel, IBM, Boeing, Caterpillar, Dana, Hewlett-Packard, Johnson & Johnson, Delta Airlines, Emerson Electric, Digital Equipment, Fluor, McDonald's, Texas Instruments, 3-M, and Procter & Gamble. These traits—and others—are also exhibited at Schlumberger: (1) "Staying close to the customer," (2) "A bias for action," (3) "Autonomy and entrepreneurship," (4) "Productivity through people"—giving all employees a sense that they count and share in the company's success, (5) "Hands-on, value driven"—promoting from within and developing one or two important corporate values, (6) "Stick to the knitting"—avoid becoming a conglomerate, (7) "Simple form, lean staff," and (8) "Simultaneous loose-tight properties"—fierce competition combined with tolerance of different opinions from colleagues who share the same corporate values.

To isolate the specific reasons for Schlumberger's success, one needs to start where Conrad and Marcel Schlumberger did—with technology. Competition in the oilfield-service business hinges on technology. Accurate geological measurements are crucial to an oil company that is about to spend millions of dollars drilling a well. Marvin Gearhart, president of Gearhart Industries, an aggressive domestic competitor of Schlumberger, says, in reference to the industry and Schlumberger, "It's a high-technology business, and they've been the leader in high technology." Riboud consistently pushes the company to maintain that lead. Schlumberger spends more money annually on wireline research and development than the total wireline profits of any one of its competitors, and John Hayward, Jr., wrote in August of 1981, "If its nearest competitor were to spend the same dollar amount, those expenditures would amount to roughly 25 percent of that company's sales."

American corporations often tend to be preoccupied with short-term results, such as quarterly profits, and this preoccupation has been noted in more than one attempt to explain the collapse of the American automobile and steel industries. A recent study by McGraw-Hill revealed that in 1982 American companies planned to invest only 3.8 percent of their revenues in research and development—down from 7.2 percent in 1980. This drop is explained in part by high interest rates and the recession. But a number of studies, including the book *Minding America's Business*, by Ira C. Magaziner and Robert B. Reich, have demonstrated that this pattern persists even in robust years. Schlumberger, on the other hand, has increased its real investment in research and engineering every year; for example, it went from $240 million, or 4 percent of its revenues, in 1981, to $326.5 million, or 5 percent of its revenues, in 1982—a rise of 36 percent. A memorandum prepared for the Schlumberger executive committee in February of 1982 says that the money spent on research in 1982 could climb in three years to $500 million. John Hayward, Jr., analyzing Schlumberger's wireline business, reported that 25 percent of the company's wireline revenues for 1980 were derived from "services introduced in the last five years." Since Schlumberger acquired the Fairchild

Camera & Instrument Corporation it has dramatically augmented the company's research budget, from $50 million to $105 million—a rise of 110 percent. Nor has Schlumberger skimped on investing in fixed assets to improve manufacturing efficiency and product quality. Despite the recession, the company's overall investment in improved productivity remained at $1 billion in 1982; at Fairchild the figure rose by $188 million.

Technologically, Schlumberger's near-monopoly of the oilfield-service industry has so far gone almost unchallenged, but now Gearhart—which has about 10 percent of the world wireline market—has vowed to change this. Almost a fifth of Gearhart's stock was recently purchased by the General Electric Company, which is still smarting from Schlumberger's acquisition, in 1982, of Applicon, a Massachusetts computer-aided-design-and-manufacturing company. GE, which owned 23 percent of Applicon, was taken by surprise when Schlumberger moved in. Schlumberger officials see an element of revenge in GE's recently announced plans to invest part of its research-and-development funds—which total $1.7 billion annually—in joint research projects with Gearhart. And Roland W. Schmitt, a senior vice-president of GE, has candidly stated that GE hopes to increase "Gearhart's penetration of traditional Schlumberger operation areas." The great companies usually spend great sums on research, a principal reason GE has thrived. So, too, with IBM, which pumps an even larger percentage of its revenues into research—a total of $3 billion in research, development, and engineering in 1982.

Despite increased effort by GE, many independent oil analysts nevertheless believe that Schlumberger is widening its technical lead. Elizabeth Taylor Peek, a vice-president and associate director of research at Wertheim & Company, the investment-banking firm, wrote to her clients on October 6, 1981, "The long-term growth outlook for Schlumberger is dependent on the continuing evolution of the wireline product, and it is excellent. Nowhere in industry is productivity improvement more essential than in the oilfield." Only a third of what is estimated to be more than 400 billion barrels of known oil in the United States has been recovered, she noted, adding, "Imagine if you increased that recovery to one-half?" (This opportunity, however, will have to wait for the current oil glut to pass.)

There will be new technological breakthroughs, according to Michel Gouilloud, the vice-president in charge of research at Schlumberger's principal research laboratory, in Ridgefield, Connecticut. "I think the main thrust for the industry will be to improve production," he says. "Now, for every hundred barrels of oil found, thirty are produced and seventy are left behind. So, obviously, if we improve that efficiency by ten percent it improves the reserves available." To improve efficiency, says Jean-Claude Picard, a vice-president who was the director of Schlumberger's research facility in Clamart, smaller equipment must be devised. Such equipment, Picard says, "would provide more measurements and reduce logging time." And the key to smaller equipment, he thinks, is the tiny microprocessors being produced by Fairchild, in California.

Helped by the Fairchild subsidiary and by a heavy investment in what is called artificial intelligence, Schlumberger may be nicely positioned for the future. In recent years, advanced technology has brought about an explosion of the well-log data that are generated at every well site. Concurrent advances in data processing have helped cope with this explosion. But an isolated field engineer cannot quickly interpret so much data, and none of Schlumberger's forty-four data-processing centers—which may be hundreds, or perhaps even thousands, of miles away from an oil well—can entirely replicate the skills of a trained field engineer. Consequently, a bottleneck has formed in the oilfield-service industry, with clients desperate for all possible information before they make their expensive decisions, and logging companies unable to provide a complete on-the-spot analysis of their complex logs.

Enter the new world of artificial intelligence, which means, according to Philip K. Meyer, a vice-president of F. Eberstadt & Company and a recognized expert on the subject, a computer capable of reproducing "the same knowledge base and reasoning processes of inference, intuition, induction, and deduction utilized by the human expert." Already, such computers have been used to speed assembly-line production, to improve medical diagnoses, and to facilitate weather forecasting. Soon they will be used to improve oil-well logging. The importance that Schlumberger attaches to this technology was heralded in a speech that Riboud, who rarely makes such appearances, gave to the New York Society of Security Analysts in March of 1980:

> This technical revolution—artificial intelligence— is as important for our future as the surge in oil exploration. It will force us to design new tools, it will change the capabilities of our services, it will multiply the effectiveness of our instruments. It will change the order of magnitude . . . of our business.

Schlumberger guessed early that artificial intelligence would be a growth industry, and jumped ahead of its competitors. According to Wall Street analysts, it is widening its early lead. Schlumberger introduced the first artificial-intelligence tool into the oilfield in 1982. Called a Dipmeter Adviser, it is connected to a computerized data base and automatically performs the interpretation functions of an engineer. Fairchild, which was once a premier semiconductor company but then lost some of its best people, is the nucleus of an effort to forge ahead in artificial intelligence. Moreover, Schlumberger has recently acquired four smaller high-technology firms (Applicon among them), and the company now has a sizable investment in artificial-intelligence research at its research center in Ridgefield, and at Fairchild's research lab, in Palo Alto. Although the extent of the investment is a closely guarded secret, Meyer estimates that Schlumberger devotes to artificial-intelligence research "a PhD-level staff of some thirty persons in addition to considerable technical-support staff." To get an idea how large this commitment is, one must consider that each year only about twenty graduate students in American universities receive PhDs in artificial intelligence. These facts lead Meyer and others to rank Schlumberger among the world's six leading non-Japanese companies in artificial-intelligence research. The others are Bell Labs, IBM, Texas Instruments, Hewlett-Packard, and Xerox.

Schlumberger's reliance on research and technology suggests a second reason for the company's success: Schlumberger executives are trained to think in ten- and twenty-year cycles. According to a survey made by the management-search firm of Heidrick & Struggles, in Chicago, and reported in the Los Angeles *Times*, 760 out of 1000 top American executives surveyed said that companies were preoccupied by short-term considerations: quarterly profits, dividend statements, this year's budget crunch; acquiring new companies without expanding basic business or productivity; hanging on to familiar but shrinking markets or to outmoded manufacturing processes. According to William J. Abernathy and Robert Hayes, of the Harvard Business School, American companies are dominated by a generation of managers who were trained in business schools, and many of them are risk managers rather than risk-takers. Indeed, an estimated 40 percent of America's largest corporations have chief executives with backgrounds in law or finance; in 1950, only 13 percent did. This contrasts with Japan, writes Robert B. Reich in his 1983 book *The Next American Frontier*, where "more than

65 percent of all seats on the boards of Japanese companies are occupied by people trained as engineers . . . Thus, in Japan, many problems that arise in business are viewed as problems of engineering or science, for which technical solutions can be found. In present-day America, the same problems are apt to be viewed as problems of law or finance, to be dodged through clever manipulation of rules or numbers."

That is not the pattern at Schlumberger. "The time horizon there is longer than that of any other company I know in being willing to wait for a return on their investment," says Felix Rohatyn. Riboud thinks his employees fall into a trap when they nervously question him about Fairchild or the drop in Schlumberger's stock price. The "fundamental question," he says, is "Where will Schlumberger's earnings be five years from now?" This willingness to take the longer view preceded Riboud at Schlumberger. It is, Riboud thinks, part of the company's "genes." Before Paul Schlumberger would stake his sons in business, he had Conrad and Marcel sign a covenant in 1919 stipulating that "the interests of scientific research take precedence over financial ones." Apparently, father did not have a hard sell. "When I was a child," recalls Anne Gruner Schlumberger, the seventy-seven-year-old daughter of Conrad, "my father told me, 'You must not forget, Annette, if we ever have money it will bring responsibility. Money is earned with great difficulty, and you are not allowed to waste it for yourself. Never.' We never spent money on fur coats or jewelry. Never, never." To this day, one of the world's wealthiest women lives in an unpretentious flat across from the Rodin Museum in Paris; she could pass for the maid as she opens the door for a visitor, wearing no makeup, a simple black wool sweater with a tissue stuffed in her sleeve, and prepares her own coffee and croissant. Gruner spends her spare time as a volunteer, helping organize children's libraries in conjunction with the Socialist governments of France and Greece, of which she approves. Her sister Dominique de Ménil, who is three years younger, is better known, probably wealthier—and no less modest. Admittedly, such unconcern for material things is a luxury success allows. Nevertheless, Schlumberger has typically thought ahead.

Riboud points out that after the Compagnie des Compteurs was acquired, in 1970, it took Schlumberger seven years to transform it into a success. "We could afford to take the seven years, because we had our basic business," he says. "If it had been ten or twelve years, though, people would have lost faith in what we were doing." The Compagnie des Compteurs is actually one of relatively few companies that Schlumberger has acquired: fifteen or so over the past twenty years—a tiny number for a company of such size and cash reserves. This is in marked contrast to the current trend among American corporations. Between 1978 and 1982, American corporations spent an estimated $258 billion to acquire other companies, many of them in unrelated fields.

This unwillingness to engage in the mergers and acquisitions game sets Schlumberger apart in a third way. Lured by the promise of size, too many American corporations have refused to "stick to the knitting," in Peters and Waterman's phrase, and have played the game with a vengeance. Whales in one industry gulp smaller fish in another, and later have difficulty digesting them. Standard Oil of Ohio spent $1.8 billion to acquire the Kennecott Copper Corporation, which has since laid off employees and piled up deficits. U.S. Steel plunked down $6.7 billion to acquire Marathon Oil, and found itself so pinched for cash that it placed its Pittsburgh headquarters building on the market. Du Pont expended $7.5 billion of its chemical fortune to acquire the Conoco Oil Company in 1981. This purchase drove its corporate debt to $7.3 billion, its debt-to-capital ratio to 42 percent, and lost Du Pont its valued triple-A credit rating. Mobil Oil, one of the first oil companies to branch out, was confident it could bring its skills to the retail business, and decided to acquire Montgomery Ward. They have so far failed to turn that company around. The Allied Corporation, which started in the chemical business and moved to oil, gas, and electronics, in 1982 ingested Bendix, a major supplier of auto parts, aerospace systems, and machine tools. The value of this merger was pegged at $2.3 billion. It was not designed to save a failing company, nor to improve productivity. Its economic justification remains to be proven. What it did succeed in doing was to drain enormous sums of money from already-strained credit markets, driving up Allied's debt by $2 billion; it provided Bendix executives with an opportunity to vote themselves "golden parachutes" in case they are deposed, including a $4.1 million severance contract for since deposed chairman William M. Agee; it inflated the true value of Bendix stock; and it generated an estimated $20 million in fees for the investment banks that advised Allied, Bendix, and the other players in this soap opera.

There are, of course, exceptions to this trend; successful companies like Beatrice Foods or Schlumberger that acquire smaller companies and diversify experimentally; or conglomerates that have succeeded at the mergers and acquisitions game. One thinks of such post–World War II empire builders as Charles B. (Tex) Thornton of Litton Industries, and Harold S. Geneen of the International Telephone and Telegraph Company, both of whom did not "stick to the knitting" and nevertheless (at least for a period of time) created leviathans. Or, more recently, of Harry Gray of United Technologies. In 1972, the year after Gray left Litton Industries, United Technologies had revenues of $2 billion, all of it concentrated in the defense industry. By 1981, this Hartford, Connecticut, firm had acquired Otis Elevator,

Carrier Corporation (air conditioners), electronic and automotive products, as well as defense-related companies, pushing United Technologies' revenues to almost $14 billion. It is now America's twentieth-largest industrial corporation and number-two defense contractor.

On the other hand, Schlumberger has not assumed that because it was successful in one field it could succeed in unrelated fields. Schlumberger, Riboud says, will not engage in an unfriendly takeover of another company, believing that the hostility generated poisons the corporate atmosphere required for success. Profit is not Schlumberger's sole criterion in the matter of takeovers. The company is "not interested in a 'financial acquisition,' " says Arthur Lindenauer, Schlumberger's executive vice-president for finance. "We acquire companies only if the acquisition represents an expansion of our basic business." And Schlumberger, Riboud told the New York Society of Security Analysts, has but one business:

> From the first day, Schlumberger technology was to collect and to interpret data, basically physical parameters. It happened that the first data we collected, the first data we interpreted, were on an oil well, propelling us in the oilfield service. Historically, it was almost by accident. Today, it is clear that there is a common thread, a common technology to all our undertakings. We are involved and committed to collect, to transmit, to compute, to analyze, to interpret data. It is the case in an oil well . . . It is the case for the new parameters to enhance drilling efficiency and safety. It is the case for collecting and analyzing voltage measurements in the electricity-distribution system to operate fast protection devices. It is the case for the sophisticated Fairchild automatic test equipment.

It is not, however, the case with all Schlumberger companies: Forex Neptune is an oil-drilling concern that owns rigs; the specialty of Dowell Schlumberger (a pumping-and-cementing company owned jointly by Schlumberger and Dow Chemical) is well stimulation. Nevertheless, an advantage that Schlumberger maintains over its wireline competitors is that virtually all of them are so diversified that their wireline divisions can't command the primary attention the Wireline gets at Schlumberger. Forty-five percent of Schlumberger's revenues come from its Wireline division, whereas its closest worldwide wireline competitor, Dresser Atlas, contributes just 12 percent of the $4.1 billion in revenues generated by its parent conglomerate, Dresser Industries, which builds compressors and turbines, is in construction and mining, and also makes refractory and industrial-specialty products. This leaves Schlumberger in an enviable position: although a conglomerate like Dresser actually has the resources to compete with Schlumberger's investment in technology, it lacks the internal pressure, and thus the willingness, to divert funds in an effort to catch up, while a smaller company like Gearhart Industries, which does devote itself to wireline work, does not have sufficient profits (Gearhart netted $31 million in 1981) to mobilize the resources necessary to catch up.

Schlumberger's determination to stick with what it knows best contributes to a fourth reason for its success: it is relatively unburdened by debt. Unlike, say, Du Pont, which had long-term corporate debts of $5.7 billion in 1982, Schlumberger's long-term debt as of December 1982 was a mere $462 million; moreover, it had a readily available cash pool of $2.3 billion in short-term investments. Such a balance sheet, says Elizabeth Taylor Peek, of Wertheim & Company, is "incredible for a company of that size." Interest income alone brought Schlumberger $254 million in 1982. In 1981, only 6.2 percent of Schlumberger's total capitalization was long-term debt, whereas the average among American manufacturing, wholesale, retail, and mining concerns has been estimated by the Conference Board, a business-research organization, to be 27 percent. Schlumberger's long-term-debt-to-equity ratio in 1981 was a mere 6.6 percent, compared with the Conference Board's average of 38 percent. The absence of debt permits Schlumberger not only to avoid onerous interest rates but also to avoid diluting the worth of its stock by selling new stock to finance expansion plans; to finance all capital expenditures with internally generated funds, and thus act as its own banker; and to acquire companies in related fields. On the other hand, as interest rates fall, the danger of such a conservative financial-management policy is that Schlumberger will sit on its cash reserves, earning less from its short-term investments than it might on business investments.

Schlumberger is exceptional in a fifth way: it is in good standing in the Third World. Multinational companies are often resented by Third World nations, which fear that their wealth has been monopolized and exploited. François Mitterrand captured that resentment in his 1975 memoir, *The Wheat and the Chaff*, recently published in the United States. Mitterrand writes:

> Zorro is coming. Zorro is already here. Contrary to legend, his manners are so discreet and his step so stealthy that no one even turns his head when Zorro walks down the street. What is he doing? He is buying. Everything. Anything. At the rate he is going, he will soon have bought up the entire collection of enterprises that go by the name of France . . . Do you think I am writing a children's story, or the lyrics of a popular song? The Zorro to whom I'm referring is the arrival on the scene of a phenomenon as important in history as the birth of nations: the advent of the multinationals. Thirteen of them are among the fifty top eco-

nomic entities of the world. If you extrapolate from the tendency we have seen happening from 1960–1968, some sixty companies, three-quarters of which are American-controlled, will by 1985 control all the channels of power. Each of the sixty will have a business volume greater than the gross national product of a country like ours.

Fearful of "Zorro," nations have nationalized or compelled corporations to accept joint-ownership arrangements, and as a result the growth of multinational profits has slowed. Despite this trend, Schlumberger has never been nationalized; nor has it entered into joint-ownership agreements. There are several reasons for Schlumberger's standing in the Third World. "You can't nationalize a spirit or brains," Riboud says. "They could nationalize a few trucks, but what would they have? The concept from the beginning was to do everything ourselves—to manufacture the equipment and deliver the services. We never sold equipment. So how do you nationalize a service?"

Schlumberger has escaped troubles of the sort that befell many oil companies in the Middle East and the United Fruit Company in Latin America, partly because it has striven to remain inconspicuous. It does not own natural resources (oil) in any nation but services those who do. It does not engage in consumer advertising, and it does not lobby governments, so it is less of a target than the well-known giant corporations. "Many companies operate successfully all over the world," says Thomas Roberts, who went to work for IBM after graduating from West Point and a stint in the Army; left after one year to become a Schlumberger engineer; and in 1979, at age thirty-seven, became the president of Fairchild. "But those companies retain their nationality. By God, they're American. Or Japanese. Or British."

The key executives of most multinational companies

tend to be of a single nationality. For example, Roberts' former company, IBM, has twenty-three members on its board of directors, all but one of whom are American. Exxon has three non-Americans on its nineteen-member board. General Electric has only Americans on its eighteen-member board.

This has not been the case at Schlumberger. Its board was evenly divided in 1982 between French and American nationals. Four of its key executives—Roberts; Arthur Lindenauer, executive vice-president for finance; Arthur W. Alexander, vice-president for personnel; and Roy Shourd, executive vice-president of Drilling and Production Services—are American. The head of the Wireline division, Euan Baird, is a Scot; André Misk, a vice-president and the director of communications, is Lebanese; Heinz Denkl, who runs the new wireline operation in Asia, is German; Ian Strecker, who leads its North American counterpart, is British; Roberto Monti, who supervises the field operations of the Atlantic wireline operations, is Argentine. Riboud and Roland Genin, the chairman of the executive committee, are French; Michel Vaillaud, who in December became the president of the company, and Michel Gouilloud, the vice-president for research, are also French, but they live in New York and Ridgefield, respectively.

This pattern is repeated throughout the company. The 1981 annual report states, "Forty percent of the engineers recruited in 1980 and 1981 for assignment outside of North America came from developing countries. To date 24 percent of all field engineers in these assignments come from these countries." At Ras Gharib, for example, which is one of two oil camps in the Egyptian desert, across from the Sinai, Schlumberger employs thirteen engineers—one French, two British, two Canadian, one Peruvian, one Iraqi, three Nigerian, one Australian, one Austrian, and one American. Worldwide, Schlumberger employs twenty-five Egyptian engineers. Engineers are trained at some eighteen sites around the globe, and a third of their teachers are from Third World countries. Alaa Mahdi, the Iraqi engineer at Ras Gharib, says, "I don't feel that Schlumberger has any particular nationality." Riboud concedes that Schlumberger's record is far from perfect. No blacks, few women, and only one Indian executive and one Japanese executive were among the 125 Schlumberger managers attending a conference of top executives in Deauville, France, in June of 1982. "We are still a company of white men," Riboud says. That may be changing, however slowly, for Schlumberger and other multinationals. "Most American companies operating in the Third World, particularly those that have been operating there for a long period, have few Americans employed in them," says Nancy Truitt, who is the program director at the Fund for Multinational Management Education, a nonprofit organization financed by foundations, corporations, and American government contracts. Hiring local people, she explains, is generally "less expensive," and lessens political tensions.

Riboud says he agrees with Mitterrand that concentration of power in the hands of a few multinationals could be "a threat to various nations," but here he favors incremental, not sweeping, reforms: "The answer to this is that you can't set the clock back," he says. He wants nations to negotiate agreements with multinationals "on tax matters, on social matters, on trade matters, on economics and accounting matters, to allow a balance of power." He still fears narrow nationalism.

Schlumberger's willingness to shed a strictly French identity is linked to a sixth reason for its success: decentralization. It is an unusually lean company, in stark contrast to a trend among corporations to expand staffs and central management. For example, the Bureau of Labor Statistics reports that although unemployment rose between January of 1980 and December of 1982, the number of managers and administrators in the American economy increased by 9 percent. "This company has no budgeting-and-analysis section, no central-marketing, no central-manufacturing, no strategic-planning department," says Allen Klein, Schlumberger's director of taxes. "That makes it unique. It's an entrepreneurial corporation, which in itself is an anomaly. Most corporations are managerial. Here the emphasis is on profitability rather than on perpetuation of the management."

This willingness to "think small" distinguishes the best companies. For example, the Dana Corporation has a corporate staff of just 100 for 35,000 employees; Hewlett-Packard and Johnson & Johnson have no planners working at corporate headquarters. And Schlumberger has a corporate staff of 197 for 75,000 employees.

William Bufton, who managed the wireline operations in Egypt and the Sudan, had a thick book on his Cairo desk setting forth in detail the annual goals he was expected to meet as division manager. His superior specified in writing the expected profit margin, the return on investment, the share of the market, the permissible lost time on the job, the number of engineers to be recruited, and the facilities to be completed in a given year. Similarly, Bufton gave the managers who reported to him a specific set of targets, and so on down the line. These goals, however, were set in the field, not at central headquarters. A Schlumberger engineer in Louisiana was asked what he would complain to Riboud about if he had the opportunity, and he replied, "Nothing. I'd talk to my district manager."

Usually, Schlumberger engineers are sent out on their own when they are fairly young, and so early on they get a taste of responsibility and are rewarded for being aggressive and taking risks. Since Schlumberger carefully screens its engineers (eight are interviewed for every one hired), since it adheres to a policy of promoting from within, and since most of its executives started out in the field, the company is suffused with independent people. Euan Baird, who joined Schlumberger twenty-two years ago, says that young men "learn and mature very quickly. A great many people don't get that responsibility until they're middle-aged, and by then they have a fixed attitude toward life."

Schlumberger's profits swell because of these independent, take-charge people; and the people grow, too. Before he died suddenly in 1982, Larry Hinde was one of the people Riboud coveted; an individual Riboud thought could one day be president of Schlumberger Limited. At the age of thirty-four, Hinde had 4800 employees reporting to him, including a fifty-four-year-old deputy. He had been to China several times, and signed an agreement on behalf of Schlumberger with that government. On weekends in Paris he often played golf with Riboud. He earned $180,000 annually, not counting stock options he owned. Not bad for a "redneck," as he called himself, from a town in New Mexico neglected on most maps. The way Hinde dressed while working in Paris remained eastern New Mexico—light blue suit, white on white shirt, iridescent tie, brown sideburns snaking halfway toward his chin. The way Larry Hinde thought and spoke, however, was light-years removed from a provincial upbringing. "My friends and the people I know back home can't believe my wife and me," he said. "They don't recognize the way I act, the way I speak. I tend to be a little bit broader in the topics I like to discuss. When Mitterrand won the elections my in-laws called and asked—'Is Mary safe?' They knew there were 'Communists' in the government."

Larry Hinde, like many of his fellow Schlumberger executives, saw himself as a buccaneer; as much an adventurer and free spirit as the wildcatters of old. He was trained to be a risk-taker, and he understood other risk-takers. Being independent was expected, not threatening. This may explain why Schlumberger employees do not hide behind anonymous quotes when analyzing or criticizing Riboud. It explains why many do not hesitate, when asked, to acknowledge that they would one day like Riboud's job. Or why Ian Strecker said matter-of-factly about his superior, then executive vice-president Michel Vaillaud, "If someone offered me Vaillaud's job I think I'm more qualified to hold it than Vaillaud is today."

Which gets to a seventh reason for Schlumberger's success, one that might be called the pride-and-humility factor. Schlumberger engineers are usually proud and self-confident, but their superiors also attempt to instill a certain humility. Being in a service business helps—what Peters and Waterman call "staying close to the customer."

All the excellent companies they studied had a quality in common: they "all defined themselves as service businesses." The company's commitment to the customer is obsessive. Caterpillar, they report, guarantees to deliver parts within forty-eight hours anywhere in the world; it is a matter of pride for Frito-Lay route salesmen to visit customers daily, no matter what the weather; McDonald's is compulsive about cleanliness; Maytag promises "ten years' trouble-free operation" for its washing machines.

And Schlumberger, from its early days, when Conrad and Marcel Schlumberger emphasized technology and service over profits, has been a company intent on staying close to and serving its customers. One sees this in the small number of central-headquarters personnel; in the company's personnel policies; in Riboud's constant admonitions to employees not to act "like King Kong." These policies and exhortations conspire to maintain in employees a balance between pride that Schlumberger is the world's leading oilfield-service company and fear that it can easily slip. Being shifted from one corporate job to another is normal for these people; growing comfortable in a job is not. "Moving people keeps the system very much alive," says Bernard Alpaerts, who in 1981 was suddenly transferred out of oilfield services to become head of Measurement & Control—Europe. "It keeps people on their toes. When you do something for five years and you're successful, you feel you know everything. When I left drilling and oil-field services in 1981, I felt I knew everything. I had been in the oilfield for twenty-nine years. That's dangerous. As soon as you feel you have all the answers, you listen less."

Alpaerts was reflecting a deeply ingrained company attitude—an attitude that was also reflected in a speech Riboud made to a conference of all Schlumberger personnel managers, in Paris, on March 17, 1981. He began by saying that only two things threatened Schlumberger. One was a thermonuclear war, over which the company had no control. The second, he said, "is within our control: the 'demotivation' of the Schlumberger people." He recalled how enthralled he was after the war by the "freedom and creativity" of America and its businesses, and continued, "And yet in less than thirty years—within one generation—although America has the same natural resources, has still the best education system in the world, has the most innovative technical creativity, I think it is a fact that many Americans became 'demotivated.' You can notice it whether you ride in a taxi in New York, whether you shop in a department store in Houston, whether you try to cash a check in a bank in Boston, whether you travel on most U.S. airlines. Workers and employees have lost the motivation that moved America forward after the war. During the same period, an exactly opposite trend took place in the Far East, particularly in Japan . . . If I look now at Schlumberger, obviously we are riding on top of the wave, everything looks bright . . . How can we lose? Simply by letting the motivation of the Schlumberger people fade away. America fell asleep. Is Schlumberger going to fall asleep, too? . . . I am now asking you to add a new and more important parameter to your job: you are responsible for the fundamental motivation of the Schlumberger people. This is a totally new dimension to your job." Riboud added, sounding like a union organizer, "You must have and ask for a higher position in the corporate totem pole, in the salary scale."

What Riboud has called "the will to win" hints at a final reason for Schlumberger's success—what employees refer to as "the Schlumberger spirit," or what Peters and Waterman label "corporate culture."

Because it cannot be measured, photographed, tasted, smelled, reduced to paper, PERT chart, or Harvard Business School formulas, analysts often overlook the role that commonly accepted attitudes, values, spirit—"the way we do business here"—plays in determining a company's success or failure. It is, for example, no secret that in Jewish culture education has traditionally been revered. In devastated slums, on the other hand, the peer-group culture sometimes lionizes the school dropout and dismisses the studious as "square." Among some, there arises what Oscar Lewis referred to as "a culture of poverty." New Yorkers can see the entrepreneurial spirit driving Koreans to become kingpins of the fruit and vegetable outlets. Countries develop a national character—German militarism, British pluck—as do sports teams. Vince Lombardi's Green Bay Packers and Red Auerbach's Boston Celtics were imbued with a special drive, pride, team spirit, will to win—a culture that set them apart.

Like countries, ethnic groups, or sports teams, companies also develop cultures. "Just as tribal cultures have totems and taboos that dictate how each member will act toward fellow members and outsiders," wrote *Business Week* in October 1980, "so does a corporation's culture influence employees' actions toward customers, competitors, suppliers, and one another." IBM's slogan—*Think*—seeks to induce employees to be problem-solvers. PepsiCo transformed its corporate attitude from passive acceptance of its rank as number two behind Coca-Cola to declaring war on Coke. According to the *Business Week* article on corporate cultures, one of the first on the subject to appear in a general circulation publication, PepsiCo chairman Donald M. Kendall took a snowmobile to work in a blizzard to demonstrate the dedication to work he expected of employees. To develop aggressiveness, Pepsi hired physical fitness instructors and promoted one-on-one and team sports contests among employees. "But," said *Business Week*, "the aggressive competitor who succeeds at Pepsi would be sorely out of place at J.C. Penney Company, where a quick victory is far less important than building long-term loyalty." At Penney, the average executive tenure was thirty-three years; at Pepsi, ten. Braniff Airlines changed the uniforms its flight attendants wore, the color of its airplanes, its marketing strategy. But it did not alter or create a strong company culture, and when government regulations expanded and competitors received the same routes, Braniff was squeezed out of business. Delta Airlines, on the other hand, confronted the same competition and government regulations Braniff blamed for its demise. Delta thrives, say Peters and Waterman, in part because its corporate culture instills the importance of teamwork, of service to the customer and dedication to the company as family.

The nature of a business helps shape the culture. A company in the consumer product business may place a premium on amiability, while a computer company prizes technical prowess. At one company the salesman is king, at another the scientist. IBM is known as a highly structured company where employees are addressed as "Miss" or "Mr.," and loyalty, discipline, and team play are valued. Schlumberger, like others in the oil business, is more free-wheeling and entrepreneurial, reflecting the nature of the oil adventure.

There are, of course, tensions at companies like Schlumberger. Employees are encouraged to be entrepreneurs, yet to work for the customer; to be competitive, yet secure; to strive for their own advancement, yet to worship a higher god—Schlumberger. Although the techniques vary, the best companies usually succeed in creating a sense of community, of being democratic. Employees feel they have a voice. In William G. Ouchi's bestselling book, *Theory Z: How American Business Can Meet the Japanese Challenge*, the author argues:

> The first lesson of Theory Z is trust. Productivity and trust go hand in hand, strange as it may seem. To understand that assertion, observe the development of the British economy during this century. It is a history of mutual distrust between union, government, and management, a distrust that has paralyzed the economy and lowered the English standard of living to a dismal level.

Japanese companies thrive because of their ability to create a sense of intimacy, a quality Ouchi says is missing at many American companies:

> In American life, intimacy has traditionally been found in the family, the club, the neighborhood, the lifelong friendship, and the church. Yet all of these traditional sources of intimacy, or primary contact with others, are threatened by our present form of industrial life . . . We resist the idea that there can or should be a close familiarity with people in the workplace. "Personal feelings have no place at work" is the common feeling. Yet we are faced with an anomaly. In the Japanese example, we find a successful industrial society in which intimacy occurs in the place of work as well as in other settings . . . A Theory Z culture has a distinct set of such values, among them long-term employment, trust, and close personal relationships.

Of course, such values did not prevent the J.C. Penney Company from slipping from its perch as America's number-two retailer; too much job security, as witnessed at Penney or in the civil service, can induce complacency. The best companies, however, manage to instill these shared values. To facilitate communication, some build campuslike corporate headquarters with parks and tranquil settings, as PepsiCo, Procter & Gamble, Kodak, and others have done. Some conduct weekly rallies and dispense badges and pins to the sales force, as Tupperware does. Some shut the executive dining room. Some have company picnics, name tags with only first names, or insist that all doors be open. What they all do is treat employees with respect. They all recognize, write Peters and Waterman, "the rock bottom importance of making the average Joe a hero and a consistent winner." Of course, this can produce an inbred company of Babbitts. Nevertheless, a good company sets goals for its employees, making them feel like achievers. If the sales quotas, for example, are too high, the bulk of the sales force will come to think of themselves as losers. It is all tied up with expectations and self-confidence. Just as a teacher better succeeds when his or her expectations are high and students come to believe in themselves, so it is no different in a corporation. A good company strives for a sense of community. It simultaneously makes employees feel that they count as individuals and are unfettered, that they are part of a clan, a family, a . . . religion.

Riboud, not surprisingly, likens the Schlumberger spirit to a religion. "It is our greatest asset, our unique strength," he says. The reason the Japanese have done so well, he told the New York Society of Security Analysts in March of 1980, is so simple and so obvious that it has been overlooked. It has less to do with their technological prowess, their productivity growth, the assistance they receive from their national government, than with spirit. "They had the same faith that the great religions had in past centuries," he said. Riboud then tried to define what makes up the Schlumberger spirit:

(1) We are an exceptional crucible of many nations, of many cultures, of many visions; (2) We are a totally decentralized organization . . . ; (3) We are a service company, at the service of our customers, having a faster response than anybody else; (4) We believe in the profit process as a challenge, as a game, as a sport; (5) We believe in a certain arrogance; the certainty that we are going to win because we are the best—arrogance only tolerable because it is coupled with a great sense of intellectual humility, the fear of being wrong, the fear of not working hard enough.

Where does this spirit come from? Surely—in part, at least—from the personalities at the top: from the Schlumberger brothers and from Jean Riboud. "Conrad and Marcel created this spirit of friendship and honesty, and Riboud kept it," says Anne Gruner Schlumberger. "Riboud is loved because he is very friendly. It is the love of people, and the interest in their life. When people left for America and Russia, Conrad escorted the engineers to the railroad station to give them advice. He knew their families, their children." The brothers communicated shared democratic values within the Schlumberger hierarchy, as Riboud does today.

The company's spirit also comes in part from the special nature of Schlumberger's business. From the start, Schlumberger has been the only wireline company to refuse to turn over raw data to clients, insisting that it alone must process these data, for it is producing a service, not a commodity. Anne Gruner Schlumberger has written that "the high quality of human relations" at the company "took its start from a 'noble' activity, in the sense that nothing produced there was mere merchandise." She goes on, "The object conceived and made there was not such as fall into an anonymous market and in their turn become anonymous. This sonde, that galvanometer, were not for sale. The tie between the man who makes and the thing made was not cut." The Schlumberger brothers stipulated at the outset that the company would not own oil wells or permit employees to buy shares in oil companies. If Schlumberger was to be trusted to keep oil-company secrets, it had to be "pure." Dominique de Ménil, another daughter of Conrad's, who was trained as an engineer and worked closely with her father, says, "You had to be totally honest, and independent of any interest." Engineers at Schlumberger sensed that they were embarking not just on a career but on a calling. They were not just merchants but missionaries.

In this sense, as Riboud says, the spirit is in the company's "genes," transmitted from the top down, starting with the Schlumberger brothers. But the spirit also rises up from the bottom. As the company grew, so did the number of engineers. Few of them knew Marcel or Conrad or Riboud. Like military recruits who go through basic training together, they became a clan. They worked sometimes seven days a week for two straight months. They lived, ate, drank, showered, watched video cassettes, and vacationed together. They swapped stories about their work. For months at a time, the only people they had contact with worked for Schlumberger or for an oil company. "It is a kind of Mafia," observed Claude Baks. One that draws strength not from the words of Jean Riboud, but from intangibles, including pride, arrogance, the sport of competition, and a sense that they, not just Jean Riboud, are running the company.

"We are proud to be the best wireline service company in the world, and when you are the best you always have the right spirit," said Larry Hinde before he died. "It was the same spirit I had when I played football and basketball. When you are winning you feel proud." A losing team has difficulty maintaining its spirit. Whether Schlumberger could maintain that spirit and pride if its profits shriveled, or whether it can transmit that spirit to acquisitions such as Fairchild, is an open question.

12

STRIVING FOR PERFECTION

How to maintain and spread the Schlumberger spirit is a preoccupation of Schlumberger executives pondering the company's future. It's not difficult to understand what has made the company so successful, Bernard Alpaerts says: "decentralization and creating a certain spirit." The danger, he says, is in "not understanding how you keep that." He worries that Schlumberger may be losing its spirit: "You can hire a young engineer today and the first question he asks is 'What's my pension?' Twenty years ago, he would not have asked that." In Alpaerts' mind, the spiritual decline is a product of the materialism, insecurity, and weakened bonds of trust that plague industrialized society.

In the view of Claude Baks, who was hired by Marcel Schlumberger as a field engineer in 1946, the company lost some of its spirit when it began acquiring additional companies and spread out of the oilfield services. "For me, the spirit has changed," he says. "Then the company was small and had a more adventurous spirit. Now it is large and has absorbed a lot of small companies that have nothing to do with oil wells. The spirit has changed, but not so much in the oil part. For the time being, it's preserved—I'd say eighty percent."

It is not clear whether the spirit is dependent on constantly rising profits. If the oil industry continues to contract, could Schlumberger employees lose their self-confidence? *The Wall Street Journal* in 1983 reported, for example, that the Polaroid Corporation was "going through a midlife crisis"; slowed growth had drained some of its creative excitement. Schlumberger executives worry that the company will divide between the robust Wireline division and the struggling Fairchild; that weaker parts of the company will pull down the strong; that executives may be transferred to divisions where their performance cannot measure up. Ian Strecker, the head of Wireline operations in North America, asserts that the Schlumberger spirit can be extended to new subsidiaries, as he believes it was to Dowell Schlumberger, where he, coincidentally, served as president. Only a third of Dowell Schlumberger's employees are engineers, he says, yet their drive has helped the company gain 35 percent of the world market. Asked whether the spirit could be imparted to the employees at Fairchild, Strecker said, "I could be wrong, but I think the answer to that is no. I think it is difficult to transfer spirit outside an oilfield-service company. We've tried it in our manufacturing plant here in Houston. There is a little bit of spirit there, but you don't get the same spirit you do in the field."

That is one cloud on the Schlumberger horizon. Another is the problematic future of the oil business. The year 1982 was brutal to most companies that make their living from the sour-smelling liquid. Worldwide, oil production declined 8.7 percent between June of 1981 and June of 1982. In North America, the number of operating oil rigs was reduced by 40 percent within eight months—from 4700 in January of 1982 to 2680 that August. (The number was down to 1990 in March of 1983.) This decline in production mirrored a decline in demand—down from 65 million barrels of oil consumed daily in 1979 to 57 million in mid-1982. The price of oil had dropped from $40 a barrel to $34 in 1982, and by mid-1983 dropped again, to below $29. Early in 1983, deep fissures in the Organization of Petroleum Exporting Countries appeared when some countries lowered their prices. Although oil prices have dropped, the cost of extracting oil is steep, and inflation and interest rates remain high. These economic factors are reflected in the profit-and-loss statements of companies connected to the oil business. In 1982, the net income of most fell. Many were compelled to lay off workers; for example, the Hughes Tool Company, a Schlumberger competitor in the drilling business, had cut 10 percent of its work force by June. New investments in research and fresh efforts to extract more expensive shale, offshore, and tertiary oil—a principal reason that President Carter decided to decontrol oil prices in 1979—dwindled. Schlumberger embarked on a major cost-cutting effort—reducing its employees from 85,000 to 75,000—and ended the year as one of the few oil-related firms with increased profits, its net income having risen 6.5 percent over 1981 (although in the last two quarters of 1982 and the first quarter of 1983 net income has dropped).

What does all this portend for the future of oil and of Schlumberger? The predictions of "experts" fluctuate widely. Morris A. Adelman, a well-known energy economist at the Massachusetts Institute of Technology, told the *New York Times* in August of 1982, "Oil is a static or, more likely, a declining industry." Many oil analysts predicted at the end of 1982 that the price of oil would dip five or six dollars a barrel (it did), and some have since asserted that the price of oil could drop to fifteen dollars a barrel—an event that would not only sharply reduce Schlumberger's profits but, Riboud argues, quickly lead to oil shortages. President Reagan, more optimistically, discontinued President

Carter's efforts to promote energy conservation, for he has faith that a free market will amply provide for public needs. A number of experts claim that the current oil glut is a mirage, warn of another oil crisis, and say there is a crucial need for conservation. The International Energy Agency, an organization composed of the twenty-one largest industrial nations, prophesied in October of 1982 that there would be an acute energy shortage by the end of the century, and that a shortage and a rise in prices would be evident as early as 1986.

Schlumberger officials make a distinction between the long-term and the short-term prospects of the oil industry. Riboud is moderately optimistic about the continued growth of oil profits in the long term, and therefore sides with the experts who warn of eventual shortages. He does not expect the price of oil to rise in the next two to three years, yet he is unperturbed, telling shareholders in Schlumberger's 1982 annual report, "A limited and orderly reduction in the price of oil to the $25-to-$30 level will have a minimal effect, if any, on the exploration and production . . . It will increase the demand of hydrocarbons." Even if drilling declines, he wrote, "we will improve the quality of our services and will grow faster than the drilling activity." The steadying of oil prices over the past decade has been a healthy development, he argues. "Fundamentally, the Western world owes a lot to OPEC," he says. "This business of believing that the marketplace can handle the price of crude oil is crazy. If it were not for Saudi Arabia"—which over the past several years has persuaded OPEC to regulate production—"you'd see tremendous swings in crude-oil prices." The Saudis, he says, "saved capitalism." Riboud believes that even if oil prices fall further, Schlumberger will be all right; he points out that even when drilling declined in the United States, Schlumberger Well Services—part of the North American Wireline—experienced steady profit growth.

Riboud acknowledges that serious questions loom: Can the Saudis lower production? Can the world absorb Iranian and Iraqi crude oil when it comes back on the market? Will OPEC collapse? Will crude-oil prices and production decline? Will some oil producers default on their international loans? Will the Saudi royal family be deposed? Will new fighting erupt in the Middle East, which today supplies 65 percent of the crude oil traded on the international market? Will there be technological breakthroughs that will lower the cost of oil discovery and extraction? Will oil exploration in North America, the decline of which was primarily responsible for Schlumberger's recent dip in earnings—the first in twenty years—rebound in 1983? Will the American economy and the world economy recover?

Despite these questions, both Schlumberger's competitors and independent Wall Street analysts are generally optimistic about Schlumberger's future. "They're a mighty fine company," says Marvin Gearhart. When he was asked if he thought Schlumberger was slipping in any way, Gearhart, who is not a man to waste words, replied simply, "No." Morgan Stanley's John C. Wellemeyer, whom the *Institutional Investor* in 1981 rated the best oilfield-service-company analyst on Wall Street, alerted investors to Schlumberger in April of 1982: "We particularly emphasize the appeal of Schlumberger. The stock price of this premier oil-service company will be the first to recover, in our opinion." In June of 1981, Everett Titus, a vice-president with the brokerage firm of L. F. Rothschild Unterberg Towbin, was optimistic about "the longer-term growth prospects for Schlumberger," and Eberstadt's Philip Meyer noted in a February 1982 report that the company was "technologically better equipped and more sensitive to new market opportunities than I've seen it in ten years."

Riboud expects oilfield services to remain at the heart of Schlumberger's business for the next fifty years. At the meeting of top executives last June, he spoke of the future and the past. Dressed casually and sitting alone on a stage, alternatively removing his glasses or inspecting his long fingers, Riboud's speech rivaled one by Fidel Castro in length—three hours, twenty minutes. But he did not shout or thump the podium, rather speaking slowly, softly, while glancing at handwritten notes.

He said that Schlumberger and the world were entering "a new cycle"—a cycle that would no longer feature annual earnings-per-share increases of 25 to 35 percent. He divided the years after the Second World War into three cycles. The first, from 1945 to 1970, had three elements: cheap and abundant energy; the world dominance of American business; and the Bretton Woods agreement creating an international monetary system. The second cycle, from 1970 to 1980, saw the end of cheap oil; the challenge to American business dominance, particularly from Japan and other countries of the Far East; and the collapse of gold as a single international monetary standard. These changes helped ignite the worldwide rise in inflation and interest rates. We are now living through the third cycle, Riboud said. Its features include a slowdown of the American economy; a zero growth rate in Western Europe; and a "sense that the boom is coming to an end" even in the Far East. "It is easy to be pessimistic," to warn of a "major crisis," or a "depression," to predict $12-a-barrel crude oil and the crumbling of the Western alliance, he said. "My own assessment is that we will have a deeper and longer recession than I and others once thought."

The oil business would not recover in 1982, or even in 1983, he guessed, but he thought Schlumberger's oilfield-service profits would probably continue to rise, though not as rapidly as they rose in past years. He said he expected the company's earnings per share to increase in 1982. (They did.) Assuming that there was no "economic collapse," Riboud said, Schlumberger's technological lead would help the Wireline division "return to normalcy." (In the first quarter of 1983, Schlumberger's profits dropped 27 percent from the comparable quarter in 1982—from $354 million to $258 million.)

Riboud was more guarded in his assessment of other divisions of Schlumberger. Though Forex Neptune enjoyed a 28 percent spurt in revenues in 1981, he cautioned that its revenues would decline in 1982. (In fact, they rose by 11 percent.) This would actually be "a blessing," he said, for "booms tend to hide a lot of sins." Over the past decade, Forex Neptune had raced to keep up with its fantastic growth, so problems had not surfaced, and executives had not had time to concentrate on long-term goals. Riboud said that he wanted Forex Neptune's principal goal to be to improve the technology of drilling. If it accomplished this, then it would "shape" the direction of drilling the way Schlumberger shapes the direction of logging.

Riboud reported that Schlumberger's two well-testing and well-completion-service companies—Johnston-Macco, which does business in the United States and Canada, and Flopetrol, which operates in South America and the eastern hemisphere—were well run and profitable. Johnston-Macco's revenues rose 42 percent in 1981, and Flopetrol's 27 percent. Typically, Riboud focused on future challenges. The long-term challenge for both divisions, he concluded, was to better coordinate their sales and research efforts worldwide. (In 1982, the two companies merged into the Flopetrol Johnston group, and overall revenues rose 11 percent.)

Riboud said that Dowell Schlumberger, the one joint venture that Schlumberger has participated in, had for twenty years been successful. Its revenues climbed 23 percent in 1981 (and 15 percent in 1982). Riboud would like to buy the 50 percent of this company that is owned by the Dow Chemical Company, he said, "but it takes two to marry." In any case, he said, "probably Dowell Schlumberger is the only successful fifty-fifty success story I know." He pridefully noted, however, that the responsibility for managing Dowell Schlumberger was Schlumberger's alone. The subsidiary's immediate goals, he said, should be to develop its own research component and to focus on fewer techniques and perfect those. As for the long term, he said he was unhappy that Dowell Schlumberger and Halliburton shared the lead, each claiming 38 percent of the pumping-and-cementing market; Dowell Schlumberger's goal must be to be number one.

Although the subsidiary called The Analysts had a 42 percent increase in revenues in 1981, Riboud expressed concern about its future. In contrast to ordinary wireline procedure, in which drilling is stopped and the oil company pulls the pipe from the well to allow logging measurements, the work of The Analysts is to provide logs during drilling. Riboud expressed pleasure that under the tutelage of Carl Buchholz an excellent management team had been installed in just a few years. But then he recalled a dinner at New York City's Sky Club three years before, when Buchholz and Fairchild's Thomas Roberts, both of whom had just been appointed to their posts, boasted of the miracles they would perform. "It has gone slower than they thought," Riboud said. He praised Buchholz's strategy-and-management team. "What we really need is tools that work in the wells," he said. After noting that The Analysts was not the number-one mud-logging company in the world, Riboud said he would remain dissatisfied until it was. (In 1982, its revenues declined 7 percent.)

The year 1981 was not a banner one, he said, for the non-oilfield-service half of Schlumberger—Measurement, Control & Components. The various companies operating in this division manufacture, among other products, electric, gas, and water meters; nuclear, petroleum, and industrial valves; and aircraft instruments. Revenues of this division declined 1 percent. Revenues of Measurement & Control–Europe declined 4 percent. The problems, said Riboud, were caused by the recession in the United States and Europe; by "the basic conservatism and resistance to change of our major customers, particularly the utilities," which were too comfortable with outmoded meters; by "the mosaic of countries and products we face"; and by the drop-off in the oil business. The challenge, Riboud concluded, was to slim down to discard products that did not promise to capture a larger share of the market.

Riboud said that Computer Aided Systems—one of Schlumberger's newer subsidiary groups—had an as yet unrealized potential. This group makes so-called CAD/CAM systems (for "computer-aided design/computer-aided manufacturing") that are intended to revolutionize the design, manufacture, and testing of products ranging from bolts to airplanes. Schlumberger's 1981 annual report declares, "The ultimate goal of this revolution could be a fully automated factory."

Schlumberger's acquisition of Applicon was a step toward this goal. Applicon was a pioneer in automating the design and drafting processes by using computers and TV-like terminal screens, so that engineers could test the function and durability of designs without building expensive prototypes. Riboud said that Applicon officials came to Schlumberger on their own, through a stockholder, J. H. Whitney & Company. (At the time, Whitney's managing partner, Benno Schmidt, was a member of the Schlumberger board.) Like many small high-technology companies, Applicon was starved for research dollars. Schlumberger provided capital, and in addition Riboud was able to match Applicon with an earlier acquisition, Manufacturing Data Systems, Inc., of Michigan. These companies, together with two other recent acquisitions—Benson, a manufacturer of computer-aided drafting systems, and Accutest, a manufacturer of test equipment—make up Computer Aided

Systems. (The Federal Trade Commission has so far blocked the acquiring of Accutest, claiming that it could reduce competition and create a monopoly for automatic test equipment.) "Everyone says it is one of Riboud's stupid acquisitions," Riboud told his executives. He disagreed. One day he expected engineers to rely on CAD/CAM systems the way they now rely on calculators. But he admitted that in the short term their profitability would be modest. The immediate objective, he concluded, was to instill in this division "the will to make money"—the same will that the best companies in the world, like IBM, the Digital Equipment Corporation, Hewlett-Packard, and Schlumberger, have had "from Day One."

Riboud talked about other Schlumberger divisions, concentrating on Fairchild. He reiterated his faith in a 21st-century vision of Fairchild becoming the main arch of Schlumberger. Or, as Riboud told the New York Society of Security Analysts in March 1980:

Fairchild is the keystone to Schlumberger measurement technology. In the last decade, during the seventies, three facts have dominated directly or indirectly our business. Their significance, their impact, will be even greater for us in the next decade, the eighties.

During the seventies, the price of gold increased fifteen times—from $35 an ounce to $500; the price of crude oil increased ten times, from $2.80 a barrel to $28; the price of a unit of memory in a semiconductor decreased twenty-five times, from one cent to 0.04 cents . . . Coal and oil have made the Industrial Revolution because they brought abundant and cheap physical power. Microprocessors and memory will make another revolution because they bring abundant and cheap intellectual power.

Although Fairchild's revenues slipped 12 percent in 1981 (and 6 percent in 1982), he said that if he were given the opportunity he would make the same decision—to buy the company—today. "Is it a business we want to be in? Yes." Although Riboud has acknowledged that he may have paid too much for it, he predicted at the time of the purchase that Fairchild's problems would take no more than five years to resolve (he now says seven years). He pointed out to his executives that two years remained. Riboud said he had started with "two simple objectives," which he hoped to realize after five years: "Fairchild should be one of the five top semiconductor companies in the world. Second, Fairchild must remain the leader in automatic test equipment in the world." To achieve these objectives, the parent company had poured huge sums into the modernization of Fairchild's plants and into research. "The question is: Are we modernizing or just plugging the leaks and subsidizing the operating losses of Fairchild? It's not simple to tell which you are doing." Riboud praised Thomas Roberts, Fairchild's president, and then said that the company now needed to strengthen its middle management and to learn from the Japanese how to manufacture semiconductors. Early in 1983, with few signs of success apparent, broad management changes were made at Fairchild, and operations at its South San Jose manufacturing plant were reduced.

Riboud scanned the room, laid his glasses to rest, and, summing up, said, "If we lost the drive, and fear searching for new technologies, or fear taking incredible gambles on new managers," or fear to heed the voices of "other countries and cultures, then we will become an establishment." If that happens, Schlumberger may remain powerful and profitable for the moment, but ultimately it will decline. "It's easy to be the best," Riboud has said many times. "That's not enough. The goal is to strive for perfection."

13

SHAKING AN
OYSTER OFF A ROCK

The only example of "perfection" he knew was La Carelle, Riboud said one day while walking in the woods there. At La Carelle he said he could live, and die, comfortably. As he sloshed over winding muddy trails, Riboud spoke of one day retiring from Schlumberger, where he had worked most of his adult life. He spoke with a mixture of pride and dissatisfaction that has, over the years, become a trademark. "You know what I think of the future of the next thirty years of Schlumberger?" he said. "I go from one extreme to the other. I don't know how we could miss—there's no way we could miss. We have the right business. A fool could replace Riboud and he couldn't even miss . . . I go to that extreme and to the other extreme, which is the danger of success. And the danger of success bringing complacency, bringing self-satisfaction—and we've gotten an establishment."

Riboud, in 1982, devoted more time to thinking about his succession, since he was sixty-three and had always said he would not seek to extend the mandatory retirement age of sixty-five, which he will reach in November of 1984. Recurrent rumors race through the halls of Schlumberger headquarters to the effect that Riboud will join the government of François Mitterrand, perhaps as prime minister.

Riboud says he first began thinking seriously about retirement and a replacement in July 1981, when he lay on a bed at New York Hospital with a collapsed lung. His old friend and board member Paul Lepercq was beside him, and Riboud remembers saying, "Paul, I've got all that I need in Schlumberger stock, and if I die the craziest thing you should advise Krishna to do is sell Schlumberger stock . . . without me it's still the best company in the world." Lepercq, who advises the Ribouds and much of the Schlumberger family about investments, recalls this conversation and of speaking for the first time about the eventual succession. That was when, he says, Riboud decided to reconstitute the board of directors to pave the way for a smooth transition.

The transition occupied the thoughts of many Schlumberger executives in 1982. "I have one big concern when Riboud retires, because that son-of-a-bitch is fantastic," said Carl Buchholz. "I'm not sure that I see his replacement. He's got some awfully big shoes to fill. Many of our people are extremely good managers. They're operationally oriented. Riboud has a vision of the future." Michel Vaillaud, then one of two executive vice-presidents of operations, conceded he would one day like to fill Riboud's shoes. But, he added, "Today, I'm afraid of being president." Why?

"Basically because of Riboud. For the first time in my life I feel somebody is far superior to me. I always thought I was far superior to the people I replaced."

"I became sort of a mythology," said Riboud in mid-1982. "Whoever replaces me will be pushed in a certain direction. Except a fool, an idiot, the circumstances will push them. Remember what de Gaulle said when asked, 'What after de Gaulle?' He said, 'After de Gaulle—a

traffic jam.' That's what it will be like after Riboud—
'a traffic jam!' I can think of four, five, six people in
different age groups who could become president."

Until a few years ago, the logical candidate to succeed Riboud was Roland Genin, fifty-five, then the executive vice-president in charge of all electronics. Genin
began his Schlumberger career as an engineer thirty-
three years ago. A burly man, he would not wear a suit
jacket without affixing to it his Schlumberger pin,
something Riboud does not do. Genin is a no-nonsense
executive, as gruff as Riboud is smooth. Several years
ago when Riboud confounded people by taking this
career Wireline manager and placing him in charge of
electronics, while elevating Michel Vaillaud from head
of electronics to executive vice-president of the more
profitable Oilfield Services, the whispers around the
office were that Genin was being shoved aside. He may
well have been. But Riboud was also sensitive that Genin
had to spend more time in the Paris office than on the
road because of family obligations. In any case, by
late 1982, Genin was not thought to be a prime candidate.

The leading candidate, according to those familiar
with Riboud's thinking, was Michel Vaillaud, a man
with a relaxed manner and a broad interest in history
and the arts. The knock on Vaillaud was that he was
relatively new to the company, and he did not start as
a Schlumberger engineer. Among Vaillaud's advantages were that he was older (fifty-one), and so perhaps
more mature than most rivals; that he had served in
both the electronics and oilfield-service divisions of the
company; and that his years in the French Civil Service
had honed his skills as a diplomat.

The third potential member of the "traffic jam" was
Euan Baird, forty-five, the executive vice-president of
the Wireline, who reported to Vaillaud; Baird is a former engineer and a bright, independent man, who often
plays golf with Riboud. But some board members felt

that Baird was something of an aristocrat, possessing the required self-assuredness and pride but not sufficient humility. A fourth candidate was Thomas Roberts, forty, the president of Fairchild. His fortunes, however, were linked with Fairchild's. Moreover, to make Roberts president before he succeeded at Fairchild would have violated Riboud's axiom that a corporate president, like the president of a nation, needs a consensus to rule. A fifth prospective candidate was Ian Strecker, the forty-three-year-old Englishman who heads the North American Wireline. Riboud did not know Strecker as well as he knew the others, but Strecker's job performance, shirt-sleeved manner, and grasp of technical problems impressed him and colleagues.

What these men had in common, besides ability, was that each met Riboud's test of choosing a successor from within the company. Ironically, the one outside name sometimes mentioned as a successor was Jérôme Seydoux, Marcel Schlumberger's grandson, the man Riboud fired in 1975. "In the present cards I think it will be Vaillaud," a Riboud confidant said in mid-1982. "But Riboud could change the cards. Or, if Riboud died, the family has one-quarter of the stock and could put in Jérôme Seydoux." This thought was echoed by former board member and Riboud friend Jacques de Fouchier: "It seems clear to me that Jérôme can always make a comeback. Frankly, I think Schlumberger is too big a company to be run by a member of the family. If Jérôme came back he would look like the representative of a quarter of the capital." Seydoux's aunt, Anne Gruner Schlumberger, was also cool to the idea. Although Seydoux is fifty-two, she said he is "too young." Speaking for one of the six branches of the Schlumberger family, she said, "I am very worried. The others are also worried. But Paul Lepercq assured me Jean Riboud has assured the succession."

Lepercq's assurance was correct. With the deft military-like precision employed seven years before when he removed Seydoux, Riboud sorted out the traffic jam at the December 9, 1982, board meeting in New York. Suddenly, he announced his successor: Michel Vaillaud. Typically, this decision was not made in isolation. Vaillaud was appointed president and chief operating officer, a new title. Instead of leaving the company with two divisions and with two senior executive vice-presidents, Riboud consolidated these in Vaillaud's hands. Executive vice-president Roland Genin was made chairman of the executive committee, responsible for long-range strategy and research. Euan Baird and Thomas Roberts now report directly to Vaillaud. Bernard Alpaerts was made the president of Measurement & Control worldwide, minus Fairchild. There was a major surprise: Roy Shourd, whom Riboud had removed as president of the North American Wireline and shunted off to a staff job in New York, was promoted to executive vice-president of Drilling and Production Services, reporting to Vaillaud. The final maneuver involved Riboud, and did not surprise long-time Riboud-watchers. Although Vaillaud was elevated to president, it was announced that he would continue to report to Riboud, who would remain as chairman and chief executive officer. Further, the board of directors voted to modify Schlumberger's mandatory retirement age, in order, the official announcement declared, "to provide for the possibility of Mr. Riboud continuing in the corporate leadership beyond the normal retirement age of sixty-five."

How did Riboud sort out the traffic jam? "The reality is that when Genin and Vaillaud were at the same level it was sort of a rivalry, so I had to settle it," Riboud said after the December 9 board meeting. Of Vaillaud he said, "I am absolutely cetain he'll succeed me."

As for his own plans, Riboud says they are no different than they've been for the past thirty-some-odd years. He will continue to serve his beloved Schlumberger. Asked if he might be tempted to become a minister in Mitterrand's government, Riboud becomes vague, hinting that any lesser post than prime minister would be a step down from his duties at Schlumberger. When pressed, Riboud usually parried the question with a question: No Socialist government would appoint to a major post the president of a multinational giant, *would they?* Even if Mitterrand wanted to appoint Riboud prime minister, his party would not allow it, *would they?*

Christophe Riboud says his father once shared with him the following conversation with the French president:

"Doesn't it create problems for you that I have been successful in business?"

"But you made all this money yourself!" Mitterrand replied. "You didn't inherit it!"

Near the end of a long weekend of Beaujolais and assorted goat cheeses, talk and hikes in the woods at La Carelle, Riboud was asked a final time whether he might join the government. For the first time in almost a year, he did not slam the door. "I don't know. I don't know," he said while climbing a muddy hill overlooking his 1300 acres. "To do what, and under what circumstances?" Mitterrand, he said, has never asked, they have never discussed it, and the possibility that he would ask is "remote."

If he did ask?

Many of Riboud's friends think he would be mad to accept. Reflecting this sentiment, Jacques de Fouchier says, "I think it would be stupid of him. To be one member of such a government when you are the chairman of Schlumberger is a very bad choice. Jean is much more useful as a confidant and friend of Mitterrand . . . To be a small minister in a weak government is of no interest." Riboud, says author-friend Françoise Giroud, "is much more useful for Mitterrand as head of Schlumberger." She says he is now free to offer advice, to raise funds for the Socialist Party, to grant credibility to Mitterrand's claim that he believes in a mixed economy. Today, she says, "He meets Mitterrand much more often than his ministers. I'd be very disappointed if Jean Riboud accepted an appointment, because it could only be because of weakness."

At La Carelle, these questions seem to fade in importance for Riboud. Surrounded by a symphony of trees, his boots planted in the wet earth, his collie beckoning his master forward, Riboud was asked a final question: Why does the youth movement he promotes at Schlumberger not apply to him?

Wounded, Riboud emitted an animal-like sound, one part hurt, one part provoked by the challenge, but mostly surprised and pained by the thought of leaving. His deep brown eyes narrowed and hardened as they fastened on his walking companion. But his voice was soft as he said, slowly, "To leave Schlumberger would be like trying to shake an oyster off a rock."

ACKNOWLEDGMENTS

A few words of thanks: This book owes much to the cooperation of people associated with Schlumberger. I especially want to acknowledge the generosity of Jean Riboud, who granted access to his company and home, and understood, instinctively, that a journalist is not supposed to be a salesman. This wisdom was also possessed by Jean-Claude Comert, a former French journalist now employed by Schlumberger, who helped steer me past several detours. Schlumberger vice-president André Misk ate roast pigeon with me in Cairo and fried catfish in New Orleans, and opened corporate as well as culinary doors. Rick Shapiro, a graduate student at Princeton, volunteered free hours to help dig up facts.

This book emerged from conversations with William Shawn, the editor of *The New Yorker*. Shawn encouraged my desire to explore new journalistic territory and, as always, taught me a great deal. Without fuss, Pat Crow skillfully edited the manuscript into a two-part piece. Eleanor Gould was responsible for copy-editing the pieces, and Richard Sacks checked the facts.

I am grateful to my agent, Esther Newberg, who remains a friend despite her ardor for the Boston Red Sox, and to Joan Sanger, my editor at Putnam, who believed in this book and who has been a pleasure to work with.

ABOUT THE AUTHOR

KEN AULETTA was brought up on Coney Island and attended New York City public schools and the State University of New York at Oswego. He received a master's degree in political science and public administration from the Maxwell School of Citizenship and Public Affairs at Syracuse University. He has served as a Peace Corps training instructor, and unlike most journalists has real management experience. In the mid-sixties he was special assistant to the U.S. secretary of commerce, and later was the first executive director of the New York Off-Track Betting Corporation. This experience enriched his understanding of the causes behind New York's fiscal crisis, which was the subject of his first book, *The Streets Were Paved with Gold*.

Today this award-winning journalist reaches two disparate audiences as a writer for *The New Yorker* and a columnist for the *New York Daily News*. His work has appeared in *The Village Voice*, *New York Magazine*, *The New York Times*, *The New York Review of Books*, *Life*, *Esquire*, and elsewhere. He has hosted regular programs on public television. His *New Yorker* piece on the mismanagement of New York City was the

1977 national winner of Dartmouth's prestigious Amos Tuck Business School Award for Economic Understanding. His last book, *The Underclass*, was chosen as co-winner of the *Washington Monthly*'s 1982 best non-fiction book. A third book, *Hard Feelings*, is a collection of his work published in 1980.